A defence of clichés

Nicholas Bagnall

A defence of clichés

Constable London

First published in Great Britain 1985
by Constable and Company Ltd
10 Orange Street, London WC2H 7EG
Copyright © 1985 by Nicholas Bagnall
Set in Linotron Ehrhardt 11 pt by
Rowland Phototypesetting Ltd
Bury St Edmunds, Suffolk
Printed in Great Britain by
St Edmundsbury Press
Bury St Edmunds, Suffolk

British Library CIP data
Bagnall, Nicholas
A defence of clichés
1. English language – Terms and phrases –
Anecdotes, facetiae, satire, etc.
I. Title
428'.0207   PE1442

ISBN 09 4660 50 6

Contents

Introduction 7
1 The cult of the original 11
2 Some effects of the cult 29
3 'Are you receiving me?' 43
4 'Camp' clichés 59
5 Play it again, Sam 75
6 Unfair to hacks! 89
7 ... and some nasty ones 113
8 Orwell and Partridge 129
9 Some examples 157
Notes 175

Introduction

> In all great epochs of history the existence of standards – that is the conscious adoption of type-forms – has been the criterion of a polite and well-ordered society; for it is a commonplace that repetition of the same things for the same purposes exercises a settling and civilising influence on men's minds.[1]
>
> – Walter Gropius, founder of the Bauhaus

The idea of the cliché as an inadmissible thing, to be shunned by all serious writers, is comparatively new. Indeed, there was a time when writers with any pretensions to style, far from avoiding what we would now call clichés, actually studied them.

I can already hear my reader (a gentle one I hope) muttering: 'Is he for 'em or against 'em?' Well, if there were a simple answer to that, there would hardly be a book in it. The right answer, which I hope to unfold in these pages, is – It Depends.

It depends, in the very first place, on what one thinks a cliché is, and where they lurk, and how one spots them. Here are some definitions.

The original French word, which had no pejorative associations, meant simply a metal stereotype for printing up wood engravings. The two notable things about it were that it resulted in a clear image, and that it could be used again and again. But then something which in printing had been regarded as a serviceable device became, in terms of writing, a *worn-out* device.

The Oxford English Dictionary dates its first recorded use in this sense as late as 1892: 'A stereotyped expression, a commonplace phrase' is how it puts it. The metaphor from printing is still there, while the connotation of wickedness is mild. But compare Eric Partridge, writing (or screaming almost) fifty years later. 'Clichés,' we are told, 'are instances of racial inanition.' (Be they *that* bad, doctor?) A certain animus against them, implied in 1892, has become something very much more serious.

By 1963 the case against the cliché is complete, with Myles na gCopaleen's definition: 'A phrase that has become fossilised, its component words deprived of their intrinsic light and meaning by incessant usage.'[2] Might one, without being unkind to the memory of the divine na gCopaleen, or risking accusations of pedantry, detect a mixed metaphor here? A fossil gives no light and cannot be used. Never mind; the point is that the original flavour of the word 'cliché' has shifted. The most important characteristic of a stereotype is its truth; it is recognisable as a copy of something, it is true to an original. The most obvious characteristic of a fossil is that it is dead.

So a cliché is a dead phrase that has lost its force. But I prefer the metaphor from printing. It is much more apt. For the plates wear out gradually. We say: 'This one's a bit worn, but it will do

Introduction

for a while longer', then someone else puts it up to the light and says: 'It's more worn than you think', and so on.

And just as printers' plates get worn, and have to be replaced, so do bits of language. If this were not the case, the Speaker of the House of Commons might well be talking in a ghastly debased Norman-French, while North Country backbenchers shouted at him in a version of the language of the Venerable Bede. However, the reasons why language changes are an academic discipline all on their own. It seems that the principal reason is that people make mistakes in it, but another reason is that people get bored with the words they use, and with the way they use them.

And the more prose we churn, or speeches we pour, the sooner boredom comes. It sometimes seems that we have been using up the plates so rapidly, and rejecting them so readily, that we are in danger of running out of stock.

But, as I say, it is not so simple. Meanwhile, lest anyone should think that I am proposing a more or less comic defence of the second-rate – for nowadays we do think of clichés as comic and reprehensible – let me quote Ezra Pound in one of his saner moments.

'It is as important,' he wrote, 'for the purpose of thought, to keep language efficient as it is in surgery to keep tetanus bacilli out of one's bandages.' (This was in a 1931 monograph called 'How to Read'.) He went on:

> 'Has literature a function in the State?' It has. And this function is *not* the coercing or emotionally persuading, or bullying or suppressing people into the acceptance of any one set or any six sets of opinions as opposed to any other one set or half-dozen sets of opinions. It has to do with the clarity and vigour of 'any and every' thought and opinion ... The solidarity and vigour of words ... is in the care of the damned and despised *literati*. When their work goes rotten ... when their very medium, the very essence of

their work, the application of word to thing goes rotten, i.e., becomes slushy and inexact, or excessive or bloated, the whole machinery of social and of individual thought and order goes to pot.

That, said Pound, was a lesson of history, 'not yet half learned'. Of course he was right; it was true in 1931 and it is true now, which is why *Animal Farm* is in the stock-cupboard of every secondary-school English teacher in the country, or, if it is not, it ought to be. So Eric Partridge's remark about 'racial inanition' is not so stupid after all. But I shall have a great deal more to say about Partridge later. Meanwhile, in my first chapter I want to look at our present attitude towards clichés a little more closely, and to ask how it has come about.

1 · The cult of the original

'Their ubiquity is remarkable and rather frightening.' So says Eric Partridge in the introduction to his *Dictionary of Clichés* (1940; 3rd edition, 1947).[1] Partridge was evidently worried that, at the rate people were writing and talking, the wells of English would soon cease to gush, and there would be nothing new to say, or only the old ways of saying it. He himself made matters worse if anything by producing for his *Dictionary* a list of some 2,500 phrases which he regarded as clichés and therefore not to be used in civilised company – thus threatening to reduce still further the resources of our language. It might have been better if he had labelled his dictionary 'A List of Expressions Not to be Used Too Much or they will Wear Out Too Soon', but by simply labelling them clichés, he hastened their demise.

For such is our current horror of using phrases which may

have been too often used before. Leave them, we say, to the bad writers and dull talkers. It was not always like that.

Until well into the last century, men of letters saw nothing remarkable about having a common stock of expressions or ideas, which they were not in the least frightened of raiding whenever they pleased. Nor was this attitude found only among the second-raters, the poetasters and pamphleteers. It was shared by the best poets, that is to say, those whose reputations were high in their lifetimes, and have endured till today.

Thomas Gray, author of the *Elegy*, borrowed extensively from the Greek, Latin and Italian. They were not obscure borrowings, either; every educated man (though not woman) knew the classics in those days. Not only did Gray borrow: he did so with pride. His great friendship with Norton Nicholls, an undergraduate of Trinity Hall when Gray was at Peterhouse, dated from the time they met at a party and got talking about Dante. Gray was delighted when Nicholls was able to point to the lines in *Il Purgatorio* which originated a phrase in Gray's *Elegy*. Hurrah, Gray seems to have said to himself, here's someone who appreciates my work.

By the 1880s such practices had already begun to be thought of as more or less reprehensible, so that when the critic Sir Leslie Stephen pointed out that most of Gray's poetry was made up of 'previously manufactured material' he was not being nice about Gray, who was out of fashion at that time. But Gray himself would have been annoyed if he had been alive to know that Stephen had *not* appreciated the extent of his plunderings.

Stephen's attitude persists today. In one of the sillier books written recently about Gray, Iris Lytton Sells, co-author of A. L. Sells,[2] reproaches the poet for his 'lack of inventiveness', shown in his 'habit of repeating himself, often the result of over-borrowing'. She goes on: 'Gray does . . . repeat himself often enough to support the view that the spring of poetry in

The cult of the original

him was very near at times to drying up.' Gray would not have had the faintest idea what the woman was talking about. Nor would he have understood her objection to his poetic inversions, which she dislikes because they ape Latin: 'He seems to have felt obliged to write in a classical manner. He was not, of course, alone in his addiction.'

To critics such as Mrs Sells, writing in a classical manner is nearly as bad as sniffing glue. (She is condescending enough to add: 'All this is not to say that, despite a certain poverty of style, he did not put together many memorable lines and phrases.') But they all did it. Pope learnt his craft by imitation. He plundered the ancient writers without shame, and praised Virgil for having done the same in his day. Joseph Spence[3] quotes him as saying: 'Virgil's great judgment appears in putting things together, and in his picking gold out of the dunghills of old Roman writers. He borrowed even from his contemporaries ... The *Aeneid* was evidently a party piece as much as [Dryden's] *Absalom and Achitophel*.' Pope also said: 'My first taking to imitating was not out of vanity, but humility. I saw how defective my own things were, and endeavoured to mend my manner by copying good strokes from others.'

And again: 'There is hardly any laying down particular rules for writing our language ... In most doubts, whether a word is English or not, or whether such a particular use of it is proper, one has nothing but authority for it. Is it in Sir William Temple, or Locke, or Tillotson? If it be, you may conclude that it is right, or at least won't be looked upon as wrong.'

Samuel Johnson saw nothing bad in copying others, either. Of Pope he says: 'He saw immediately, of his own conceptions, what was to be chosen, and what to be rejected: and, in the works of others, what was to be shunned, and what was to be copied.'

I will quote Iris Lytton Sells once more, before leaving her for ever. 'On the whole,' she writes, 'Gray's poetic figures are largely legacies from the past,' plainly intending this to be a Bad

Show; but for Gray, it was a Good Show, as, indeed, it is for us. For this is the man of whose *Elegy* Johnson wrote that it 'abounds with images which find a mirror in every mind, and with sentiments to which every bosom returns an echo.'

Gray's readers got pleasure from thinking he had borrowed something even when he had not. Johnson goes on: 'The four stanzas beginning "Yet even these bones" are to me original: I have never seen the notions in any other place; yet he that reads them here, persuades himself that he has always felt them.'[4] That is the secret of Gray's *Elegy*; it explains, or at least illuminates, the extraordinary power the poem has to move deeply even those who are not familiar with the literature from which so much of it is taken. It is as though there is a sort of forgotten chord in us all, which is wakened by such things; in the same way, many people who hear Beethoven's setting of Schiller's *Ode to Joy* for the first time insist that they knew it already. (This certainly happened to me; I could not possibly have heard it earlier, this being well before the tune was vulgarised by the Men of Europe.)

I shall come back to Pope and Co later when I discuss various sorts of cliché; the point I am making here is simply that two of the greatest poets in our language wrote work which was to a large degree derivative, and no one thought the worse of them for it. Yet today to say that a poet, or indeed any writer, is a derivative writer is to offer him or her an insult, and might even produce a solicitor's letter in the next day's post.

The habit of borrowing was not peculiar to the Augustans. Spenser had done it by imitating Chaucer, and as for Spenser himself, his imitators are numberless, and can be found well into the eighteenth century. Such practices were the most natural thing in the world. The education system encouraged them.

It was the same education which had been generally accepted since the Renaissance, and was based, of course, almost entirely on what had survived from ancient Greece and

The cult of the original

Rome. Thus Roger Ascham – a royal tutor and a Fellow of St John's, Cambridge, in the middle of the sixteenth century – declared that Latin and Greek were the *only* models.

> Because the providence of God hath left unto us in no other tongue, save only in the Greek and Latin tongue, the true precepts and perfect examples of eloquence, therefore must we seek in the authors only of those two tongues, the true pattern of eloquence . . .[5]

He then goes on in great detail to prescribe those classical authors who are most suitable for imitation in each kind of writing. Since both languages were dead, at least in their classical form; since what had survived of them was limited, and could never be added to (except by some lucky find); and since teachers like Ascham further limited their pupils by advising them which author to imitate on which occasion, a student who wanted to please his tutor had practically no room for originality: he could only rearrange patterns of language already coined by someone else. And Ascham went yet further, promising also to distinguish between those parts of a given author, in a given genre, which ought to be imitated and those which ought to be eschewed. Marcus Tullius Cicero was particularly admired:

> Thou that shootest at perfection in the Latin tongue, think not thyself wiser than Tullie was . . . Think not thy wit better than Tullie's was, as though that may serve thee that was not sufficient for him.

In Ascham's day there was a fashion for paraphrasing a Latin author into different Latin, which Ascham thought little of, since the Latin of the paraphrase was bound to be worse than that of the original; so he strongly recommended what he called 'double translation': the teacher puts an unfamiliar passage of (say) Cicero's into 'good plain English', the pupil translates it back into Latin, and the two Latin versions are compared. Naturally, the best pupil is he whose version is most like Cicero's. Ascham also thought that Cicero was the best model for eloquence and propriety when it came to writing *English* prose as well.

Richard Mulcaster, High Master of St Paul's at the end of the same century, was equally discouraging towards originality:

> That there is too much variety in teaching, and therefore too much ill teaching (because in the midst of many bypaths, there is but one right way) he were senseless, that sees not: if he either have taught, or have been taught himself. Which whence it springeth, diversities of judgment beware . . .[6]

In other words, stick to what's been done before.

That system was still going strong at the end of the nineteenth century. J. H. Badley, a dissatisfied pupil at Rugby in the 1880s, complained that 'at best it was a training at second hand in that it was entirely bookish, teaching us to look at everything through other's eyes rather than our own.'[7]

There had, it is true, been earlier attempts to get away from it, long before Badley started Bedales in 1893. David Williams, a Rousseau-worshipper, had set up a progressive school in 1773, having seen boys of twelve memorising bits of Ovid which they would only forget later; and early in the nineteenth century Charles Mayo, headmaster of a very unusual school at Cheam for the sons of the upper classes, declared his policy to be that 'In every branch of study, the *point de départ* is sought in the actual experience of the child.'[8]

But these were cranks. Mayo's phrase about 'actual experience' was not to become orthodox thinking till about 120 years later. As David Shayer, in his excellent study of the history of English teaching in the present century, puts it:

'Imitation' was not simply an isolated classroom exercise, but a whole way of thinking that was taken for granted by a great many teachers, if not by the vast majority, certainly until 1920 and even beyond.[9]

This was still true in my own 'progressive' public school in the early 1940s. When, like a lot of teenagers, I liked to write overblown purple passages, my wise English teacher advised me to study Lamb's *Essays of Elia*. He was really only doing what Roger Ascham recommended in his book published in 1570, when he challenged his pupils to write better than Cicero: if I was to write quaint English, I might as well follow a good model, and do it properly ...

It had, indeed, been a long tradition, and I am not saying it was a bad one. But it has gone.

What have we now? Let me quote from a symposium called *New Movements in the Study and Teaching of English*, edited by myself in 1973, which had a modest success and is, I believe, still in print.[10] Its aim, as implied by its title, was to bring together all that was best in contemporary thinking among English teachers. Ken Worpole, then head of the English department at a big London comprehensive school, wrote in his contribution:

> It is not too difficult to imagine the situation, a largely desirable one I believe, in which most of the reading material available within a school would in fact be produced by the children themselves and other members of the community.

(The latter category did not, ideally, include the teacher.) The great advantage of such a scheme, which he was pursuing in his own school, was that when the children came to write their own compositions 'The language and syntax are precisely those used by the children themselves – their key words rather than ours.'

Or take a handbook of advice for teachers, also published in 1973, called *Patterns of Language*, by Leslie Stratta, John Dixon and Andrew Wilkinson, in which the authors describe a writing course for teachers.[11] One teacher, asked to write a descriptive piece about a big city, is quoted as saying:

> I wanted to choose a picture which would relate more closely to my experience. This was the first difficulty. What kind of picture should I choose – so that I may identify with it – *my* emotions, *my* thoughts, *my* experiences?

Another teacher reported:

> When I read what I had written that wasn't the way I felt, or if it was the writing seemed stiff, stilted, phoney . . .

The authors comment:

> To have chosen an objective correlative is not to have solved one's problems: it may offer its own words, may invite a stock response . . . The cliché, whether of word or idea, simplifies and thus distorts . . . Thus an important part of the creative process is a search for words and images unique to the experience.

Unique, that is, to that particular personal experience. It may be noted that neither of the teachers (at least in the extracts quoted) mentioned clichés – but the authors do. The implication is that anything which is not the very own 'word or idea' of the writer is to be labelled 'cliché'.

Such an emphasis on personal experience was, of course, quite foreign to the Augustans. They were not interested in what they regarded as individual deviations from general truths, or, as the poet Imlac says to Rasselas:

> The business of the poet is to examine, not the individual, but the species: to remark general properties and large appearance; he does not number the streaks of the tulip, or describe the different shades of the verdure of the forest. He ... must neglect the minuter discriminations, which one may have remarked, and another have neglected, for those characteristics which are alike obvious to vigilance and carelessness.

Johnson did not mean that writers were themselves to be unobservant: like Pope, he was insistent that Nature (that is to say, the observed world) was to be carefully studied: 'No kind of knowledge was to be overlooked' by the poet. But it was not self-knowledge. The Augustans would have been much puzzled by the teacher in *Patterns of Language*, anxiously trying to discover what *he* felt about the city he was supposed to be describing. His proper aim, they would have said, should be to find out what the city was like, and to describe that. If the writer sought the answer in what he thought or merely felt he saw, he would probably get it wrong.

Rasselas, being a satire, does not necessarily reflect what Johnson thought – after all, in many ways he was well ahead of his contemporaries – but it was the wisdom of the time, the sort of thinking which had made Pope write of

> Unerring Nature, still divinely bright
> One clear, unchanged, and universal light.

Such was the gulf between Imlac in the eighteenth century and Ken Worpole in the twentieth, and it is interesting to see how it came about.

Since most education systems have a natural inertia, there was likely to come a time when the old ideas eventually went stale, as schoolteachers went on making their pupils learn by imitation long after the eighteenth-century view of the world had been superseded: in other words, when they were using the old techniques without really knowing why. This was certainly true in the two respectable preparatory schools I went to myself in the 1930s. We were supposed, for instance, to copy sentences from a text-book written in old-fashioned copperplate, of the sort you see nowadays only on visiting cards, the labels of certain wine bottles and the straplines of some classier newspapers. The knowledge gained from these exemplars (*Coal comes from Doncaster* was my own first effort at the age of about seven, and a fine mess I made of it) was quite incidental; the only aim was to make sure we executed the proper curlicues, and observed a regular slope. Exactly the same principle governed our written compositions. The information we gave in our essays mattered less than the way in which it was set out, if it mattered at all. It was best to start with a generalisation, *à la* Francis Bacon, and end, if possible, with a neat little aphorism, never mind what, and the whole composition had to be hung on a preparatory skeleton, preferably with sub-sections, showing the progress of the argument.

Shayer cites a pleasing example of this sort of thing, dating from some thirty or forty years earlier, which I cannot resist quoting. A textbook on *Junior School Composition* of 1901 requires pupils to

> Write on 'The Cat'; 1. Where found. 2. Why kept. 3. Fitted to be a beast of prey – (a) teeth, (b) claws, (c) pads. 4. Fitted for night prowling – (a) fur, (b) eyes. 5. Fitted to be a pet. 6. Habits.

The reaction to all this emphasis on imitation, which had been the grand principle of educators for so long, was inevitable sooner or later; and two things hastened it. One was the increasing availability of cheap literature and the growth of popular journalism; the other was the 1944 Education Act.

The trouble with getting as many people as possible to read, as every true democrat knows, is that you cannot be sure that they will read the right things. David Shayer quotes an essay of 1897 written by a 14-year-old girl, which was highly praised at the time:

> The present is a time calculated to arouse the warmest feelings of loyalty and patriotism in the coldest heart that ever beat in a land governed by our beloved Queen... From far-off Australia to mighty India, from rocky Gibraltar to ice-bound Canada, the glad voices of a million happy subjects come in one great hurrah...

And this from an 11-year-old in 1924:

> 'A Day at the Seaside' – what pleasure is in those words – for with them comes the echo of the waves lapping upon the golden sands... To children who live in the smoky towns the experience of a visit to the blue sea is a delightful one and one may well notice the eager looks on the faces, pinched and pale, of the slum children, as they packed into the railway carriage, bound for the seaside. Poor little mites...

Etc, etc. This was not quite what people had meant when they talked about getting children to imitate the best models. Obviously the girl had been reading a lot, but what trash! The sentiments were impeccable, of course; the phrases chosen, however, were entirely automatic. She should have been asked, like the child who has been playing in the dirt, 'My dear, where *have* you been?' The 11-year-old's sentiments are, like his language, all second-hand. He was, of course, only trying his wings, as it were. But it was this sort of stuff, among other things, which made Denys Thompson, founding editor of the influential magazine *Use of English*, write in its first issue in 1949:

> It is a commonplace now that education must educate against the environment. And yet after eighty years of compulsory education the environment seems to be winning . . . The most insidious attacks on the individual are verbal, through advertising, the popular press, cheap fiction, radio and film, with the result that most of us carry on our thinking with only the language and attitudes of Northcliffe journalism to help us. The language we use has almost ceased to be a conveyor of heritage or a means to emotional and intellectual understanding.

In the same issue, in an article under the title 'English in Exams', Robin Pedley wrote despairingly of

> the practice of the majority of examining bodies, who continue to set the one-word subjects – 'Tunnels', 'Sunday', 'Wheels', 'Forests' and the like – which invites the artificial 'essay' and stimulates among the more promising pupils that superficial smartness and brightness, that glib facility for saying nothing charmingly, that for too long has been the hallmark of the good essayist.

Some textbooks, selling in their thousands and ordered in bulk through the less progressive education authorities, actually encouraged schoolchildren to familiarise themselves with the drearier sorts of cliché, by asking them to fill in the missing words of such phrases as:
    As green as . . .
    As old as the . . .
or, for more advanced pupils:
    Lock, stock and . . .
    Hook, line and . . .
Pedley comments on such examination questions:

> If the frequent question [in the School Certificate] on 'idioms' is prepared for, such preparation must stultify any

effort to foster vigorous and sincere expression. 'To burn the midnight oil' (or 'the candle at both ends'); 'to let sleeping dogs lie'; 'to beat about the bush' are not phrases we shall be pleased for our pupils to use, yet such stale and outworn metaphors form the stock-in-trade of this question. Surely we can spend our teaching periods more profitably than in encouraging a respectful attitude to the cliché!

It is sad to think that this 'respectful attitude to the cliché' which so upset Pedley so long ago is still to be found today, though in different form. Longman's *New Generation Dictionary* (1981), which according to its blurb 'includes the language needed by today's young people', offers as examples of its definitions some distressingly banal phrases and sentences, such as:

When she saw him her eyes kindled.
The singing of the birds heralded the day.
A graphic description.
The frontiers of medical knowledge are being pushed
   further back.

All are fairly harmless turns of phrase, except 'a graphic description' (and surely the verb 'herald' needs to be used with care!); and many of the examples given in the dictionary are nearer idiom than cliché. But they are hardly worth imitating.

Anyway, from 1949 on, progressive teachers were engaged in a perpetual battle to prevent pupils from imitating bad models. Harold Rosen, one of the most prominent of them, complained in an article[12] written in 1965 how careful he had to be when setting essay subjects for homework, if he was not to get a sheaf of poor, thin stories about cops and robbers full of stage-property guns and daggers taken from pulp fiction or popular comics.

In short, by the end of the 1940s the education-via-imitation philosophy had at last begun to go sour. The difficulty was, what to do next. A new school of thought began to emerge, called by cynics the bubble-blowing school. The idea was to offer the pupils some instant frisson or other – fill the classroom with soap-bubbles, start a small fire, anything – and ask them to put down their immediate personal reactions to the happening, without the intervention of any literary or indeed any other sort of model: they would come to the experience pure and, as it were, untainted by outside influences. Teachers without bubble-blowing equipment might simply stick up a lovely big poster – say of a ship in full sail, leaning with the wind – and ask the pupils to write about that, in their own words, of course.

The technique was full of hazards. The temptation for the teacher to offer a few ideas to get the pupils going was very large, and even if he or she managed to resist it, he could not guarantee that they would not come out with images of salt and spray which were not entirely their own.

It would be unjust to Denys Thompson, or to the founders of the London Association for the Teaching of English, a notable spearhead group to which I remember belonging myself in the 1950s, to suggest that they generally fell for this sort of thing – Thompson was trying to counteract the evils of the bad literature, not to deprive people of the good – but plenty of teachers did.

Sir Alec Clegg, then chief education officer for the West Riding of Yorkshire – one of the most powerful education authorities in Britain – edited a book called *The Excitement of Writing* which had a great vogue when it came out in 1964.[13] In it he made a distinction between what he called a pupil's 'recording' English and his 'personal' English. The former might include many words and phrases 'taken not from his own store but from books recently read or notes recently taken down'. The pupil's 'personal' English, on the other hand, relied on 'his own store of words'. That was the English he or she used when writing 'poetry or expressive prose'.

Clegg was not belittling 'recording' English; indeed, part of his point was that if people were good at one kind of English they were likely also to be good at the other – but his distinction between them implies that one is 'original' and the other not; and the most important thing about 'poetry and expressive prose' was that it ought to be original.

Of course Clegg could not, if he thought for a moment, really imagine that a young writer could write well without models. Where, outside mere spoken English, would such a writer get the 'store of words', to use Clegg's phrase, which was supposed to be personal to him? The thing is impossible. In one of the very first examples he gives in his book of 'personal English' we have a 15-year-old Yorkshire boy writing:

> In my opinion, the most interesting person in our street is a coalminer. This man is about thirty-four years old and as fit as a fiddle . . .

Fit as a fiddle, eh? His own store of words? But the lad must have been pleased. He'd discovered just the right simile for his purpose . . .

Meanwhile, the progressives were gradually gaining ground, and their new spearhead group, the National Association for the Teaching of English, was being listened to seriously by the people who ran the examination system. By 1973 James Britton, a prominent member of the Association and a much-respected trainer of teachers, was able to declare:

> Authoritarian teaching has become an anachronism during the course of the past 20 or 25 years . . . The teacher's authority has still today to clear a space for learning to go on; *but* [my italics] *the learning proceeds otherwise.*

So much for Robert Mulcaster, with his 'In the midst of many bypaths there is but one right way.' If anyone was the master now, it was Rousseau's Emile.

Diversity was all. One man who did a lot to steer people's thinking in this direction was Randolph Quirk (later Vice-Chancellor of London University). There is no such thing, he pointed out, as one, single form of 'correct' English. There were many forms of correctness, according to the writer and the occasion. Fitness for purpose – not such a new-fangled notion, when you come to think of it – was what mattered. Quirk would illustrate the point by some hilarious juxtapositions, such as this from a supposed letter of thanks:

> It was extremely gracious of you to invite me, Lady Jones, and I've had bags of fun.

'Bags of fun' is not 'worse' English than 'extremely gracious'; each is wrong only in the context of the other. 'It is the height of naïvety,' Quirk wrote, 'to go round with a single yardstick, measuring English as "good" and "bad".'[14]

It was Quirk, incidentally, who gave the inaugural address to the National Association for the Teaching of English when it was founded in 1963. (The above quotation comes from his book, *The Use of English*, first published the year before.)

The next stage in the argument took teachers into paths of thought down which I doubt very much whether Quirk would want them to go. First, it was rather too easy to move from the idea of there being 'no single yardstick' to the idea of there being no yardstick at all. But if you avoid that brambly path, you might find yourself up an even bramblier one; and many did. You start with the very proper notion of fitness for purpose: one style is appropriate in one instance, another in another. You then ask: What is the appropriate style for the hundreds of thousands of children who, as the 1944 Act required, enter secondary education every year?

Before the Act, anyone who got to secondary school expected to be given plenty of English literature, and accepted the idea because it was clear that without a knowledge of English literature, attested by the Certificate, no one could enter the professional and managerial classes. After the Act, the secondary schools were full of people who had no such aspirations and were not in the least bit interested in literature. At first there was some puzzlement: what should they be taught? But once you accept the idea that secondhand experience is stultifying and personal experience is significant; and have seen what happens when the old tradition gets into the hands of second-rate pedagogues and pettifogging examiners; and begin to realise that there is more than one proper way of writing, and conclude that the best way of writing is the one appropriate to the child who holds the pen – then the way is clear. 'Their key words, not ours,' says Ken Worpole. And when you find that pupils who don't want to write middle-class English prose turn out to be very good at writing demotic prose – 'their key words' – your answer, indeed your duty, some teachers said, is obvious.

From then on the argument is really a political one, and is more or less outside my scope. Here I am interested only in what happens when the Augustan model crumbles to bits and the Cult of Originality takes its place – causing, among other things, a famous lexicographer such as Eric Partridge to write about clichés as though they were a form of dry rot, 'rather frightening' when he thinks he sees it spreading.

2 · Some effects of the cult

The idea that imitating others is bad leads insensibly to the belief that what other people have written can be ignored. Or even, if you take the extreme position, *should* be ignored. For the corollary is that every single person is, and should be, different from every other person. It follows that the best English compositions are those which indicate such differences, that is to say, those which owe nothing to anyone. All else is cliché. In this chapter I show two instances – one in the universities, the other among the architects – of this process at work.

No such notions bothered, or impinged on, the newspaper-reading public much until the student revolutions of 1968–70, when good, solid citizens, who had been brought up nicely in the old ways, began to look up from their breakfast tables with an awful sense of bewilderment. The spectacle of students defying their teachers made no sense to them. They themselves, at school or university, had been like fledglings, waiting, open-beaked, for their Alma Maters to deposit the traditional values. What was happening? How dare these students turn the world upside down? (Other solid citizens, who had not themselves been to college, were just as upset, and in fact the popular papers were far less sympathetic to the students' cause than the quality papers were.)

However, the students' leaders were not the philistines the leader-writers took them for, and could bring their own logic to the situation. After all, if you have been brought by observation to believe in the sovereignty of the individual mind, it is no longer necessary to take it for granted that your tutor's is any better than yours. Not-so-clever students attributed all this public indignation to the fact that most of the Press was controlled by the wicked Tories, but it was not to be explained in such crude political terms. Anyway, millions of words, some wilder than others, were spent in analysing the phenomenon.

Among the more interesting explanations was that put forward by A. E. Dyson, a charming and civilised man who lectured at the University of East Anglia. It was an overreaction, but it had a point. He proposed that the student revolt represented the ugly death-throes of the Romantic Revolution, no less. Dyson wrote:

> A bankrupt and dangerous romanticism is at work, with its roots in the early nineteenth century or even before.[1]

He then went on to quote, with evident distaste, Blake, Wordsworth and Keats. From such as them (the argument went) stemmed all the inadequacies of current educational theory – the importance of self-expression, the consequent reluctance to grade pupils according to their actual ability, the loss of 'rational ideals and disciplines', and so on.

The final result, Dyson thought, was 'frantic self-fulfilment divorced from reason and discipline', particularly in the context of 'pop' culture. But when one takes away from his article all the anger (and, one might add, fear) which the student rebellion provoked at the time, one sees that it is really a plea for a general return to the ideas and values of the Augustans, or at least to those of Edmund Burke, who believed that every person's perception of, and reaction to, any given phenomenon was the same as everyone else's.[2] What is beauty? Why are we afraid of the dark? It was not to be supposed that we should find the answers simply by rummaging about inside our own skulls. The right way was to analyse the nature of darkness, Burke would say; only then could we understand how the mind worked. The Romantics, on the other hand, had shifted the emphasis entirely: the centre of interest was no longer the object contemplated, but the mind which contemplated it. The rebellious students, with their belief that what *they* wanted to study was more interesting than what their teachers thought should be studied, could be regarded as embodying the Romantic idea in its extreme, degenerate form.

The thesis is by no means as dotty as it sounds, though it would doubtless have come as news to a great many dissident students who had perhaps never set eyes on a single line of Wordsworth's. William Minto and Hugh Chisholm, in their 1911 *Britannica* article, complained of Wordsworth's 'habit of taking *his own mind* as the standard of the way in which "men associate ideas in a state of excitement", and language familiar to *himself* as the standard of "the real language of men"', which was a neat way of putting it.[3] For of course, along with much of the machinery of eighteenth-century aesthetics, Wordsworth also rejected the language which accompanied them.

When we read in his preface to the *Lyrical Ballads* of the 'gaudy and inane' phraseology of many of his contemporaries, we are reminded of Myles na gCopaleen's definition in our own time of a cliché as a phrase whose words have been deprived of their intrinsic light and meaning, or of Eric Partridge, who in the introduction to his *Dictionary* talks of 'pointless metaphors' and 'fly-blown phrases'. Wordsworth was an anti-cliché man. He wanted to write about the feelings of working-class people, in what he thought was working-class language, which was less vulnerable to 'social vanity'. For he was also a revolutionary who believed in 'the essential passions of the heart' and 'the spontaneous overflow of powerful feelings'. His message is muddied and darkened with a great many Hartleianisms to do with the theory of the Association of Ideas, but its import is plain, and one can see its family likeness to the slogans put about by the student revolutionaries.

But what happened to Wordsworth when, having decided to reject the poetical devices of his age, the classical personifications, the mandarin words, and to cut himself off, as he put it, from 'a large portion of phrases and figures of speech which from father to son have long been regarded as the common inheritance of poets' – what happened when, having made this decision, he took pen in hand and started to write poetry? As we all know, he produced verses of the utmost banality, which no one reads today except reluctant schoolchildren, or students of Eng. Lit.; or if the rest of us take one of them up, it is only for a laugh.

This is not to belittle Wordsworth at his best. In his *Tintern Abbey* (which was included in his *Lyrical Ballads* collection) he showed that it *was* possible to discard the 'common inheritance' and still write poetry of miraculous power. More often, though, what we got was this sort of thing:

> Nay, rack your brain – 'tis all in vain,
> I'll tell you everything I know;
> But to the Thorn, and to the pond
> Which is a little step beyond,
> I wish that you would go:
> Perhaps when you are at the place
> You something of her tale may trace . . .

Some effects of the cult

'Tis now some two-and-twenty years
Since she (her name is Martha Ray)
Gave with a maiden's true good will
Her company to Stephen Hill;
And she was blithe and gay *etc, etc.*

How was this? How was it that 'the great and universal passions of men', which Wordsworth grandly proclaimed to be the most valuable object of all writing, could thus emerge in such broken-down, platitudinous twaddle? Well, it was only an experiment, and he knew he might fail. No doubt he reflected, to use the language of the *Lyrical Ballads*:

For sure, 'tis better to have tried
Than never to have tried at all;
The sad truth scarce can be denied,
You cannot win them all.

Wordsworth's experiment just showed the hazards of junking wholesale the 'common inheritance' and trying to start afresh with nothing but the bare bones of language. Wordsworth certainly felt passionately, but had purposely denied himself the rich means available to him of expressing his feelings, rather as those equally passionate students of the late 1960s, who likewise rejected the common (or 'bourgeois') tradition, could only exclaim that they were having a gas.

The students were like Wordsworth in another way. Just as he abandoned (for a while) the 'high' poetic style for the honest locutions of the labouring classes, so the student movement sought in its pronouncements to ally itself with trade unionism. What was needed, it declared, was 'a resolute fight against the hold which the British ruling class exercises over universities and colleges and the authoritarian system whereby they maintain it', and it added (I quote here the manifesto of the Revolutionary Socialist Students' Federation of 1968):

> The revolutionary character of the demand for student power will only be safeguarded if students reject the notion of higher education as a self-contained world of its own. Militant students must reach out to the potentially revolutionary forces in society as a whole.

It is to be noted that in throwing overboard the clichés of bourgeois imperialism, as enshrined in their traditional degree courses, these students had acquired a splendid haul of their own. Nature filled the vacuum. At least they had found some sort of a voice. The unhappy outcome, though, of all this talk of individual liberty, all this clearing of the decks, was a boring uniformity of thought, manners and dress, as drab and as featureless, one might say, as one of those dud lines of Wordsworth.

David Martin, a lecturer in sociology at the London School of Economics (generally regarded by journalists, perhaps because it was so close geographically to Fleet Street, as the epicentre of the student revolution), offered a delightfully telling comparison between the besieged universities in the 1960s and the monasteries at the time of the Reformation.[4] Just as the Protestant reformers subscribed to the priesthood of all believers, so the new protesters demanded the participation of all students. Out to 'smash' the academic hierarchy, they tried as hard as they could to avoid setting up one of their own. There must be no leaders. From the proposition that students should be able to choose what they studied, the further proposition followed that the academics could be disposed of altogether, and the students could run their own anti-universities, but since they disbelieved in any single person running anything, these brief institutions (some of them, like the gaudier sort of insect, lasted hardly more than a day) often amounted to no more than aimless talking-shops.

I mention these happenings only because they seem to me an excellent demonstration of what comes of trying too rapidly to abolish a conventional structure, and, with it, the language which supports it. Tedium rules. 'Radical students,' Martin noted, 'fear all categorisation': the invisible Church has no membership. But this reluctance to be typecast can leave the individual with no identity at all: a sadly circular outcome.

Martin, writing in 1969, also noted the Protestants' dislike of ritual and a similar dislike among revolutionary students of the conventional observances of academic life. If he had written a few years later, in the mid-70s, he would have observed what had happened to the conferences of the National Union of Students under the control of the Broad Left faction. Their debates were not concerned with the Union's policies, about which at that time there was little disagreement, but with the doctrinal correctness or otherwise, in political terms, of the manner in which the policy was proposed. 'Your analysis,' they would cry to each other, 'is correct', or incorrect as the case might be; the debates thus had a distinctly ritual flavour, and indeed had for many years before that been conducted very largely by challenges to the chair on points of order. In this sense, all the student movement had done was to substitute one set of conventions for another, and the losses were greater than the gains.

But enough of students. The point being made is that a too-hasty rejection of the traditional linguistic conventions can only too easily impoverish the mind, which is left with too little to feed on; and that the Cult of Originality can lead, in fact, to its very reverse, a distressing uniformity.

Another analogy, better in some ways than that provided by the revolutionary students, can be found in architecture. It is always rather perilous to translate the ideas of one medium into those of another, and obviously the parallel is nothing like exact, but it is pleasant and instructive all the same. One of the aims of the Modern Movement was to get away from the eclecticism and 'historicism' of the late nineteenth century, which had thought of buildings largely in terms of the style in which they should be clothed. 'A breach has been made with the past,' declared Walter Gropius,

> which allows us to envisage a new aspect of architecture corresponding to the technical civilisation of the age we live in; the morphology of dead styles has been destroyed; and we are returning to honesty of thought and feeling.[5]

What the Modern Movement was destroying, in fact, was a whole architectural language which had been used by builders for centuries, and had been perfectly well understood by anyone who stopped to look at it. To take one of a million possible examples: the pilasters with which John Wood adorned Queen Square in Bath were not put there merely for decorative purposes. They were there to tell everyone who passed by that these were important houses tenanted by powerful people, just as, shall we say, the deliberately archaic language which Malory used in his *Morte Darthur* made it clear that these were no ordinary knights and that their battles were about something that mattered. Nikolaus Pevsner said that Ruskin 'might have known better' than to identify ornamentation as the principal part of architecture,[6] but Pevsner, himself a New Movement man, was being unfair to Ruskin here. Ruskin believed that ornamentation was an *essential* part of a building, and that if it was not essential it ought not to be there. John Wood's pilasters were not structurally essential, but they were the language in which the building spoke; and it was a very old language indeed. They took their models from ancient Greece and Rome, where they did have a structural function, since they held up the roof, whereas the eighteenth-century version merely held up the cornice, itself a rhetorical device, hated with a deep, strong hatred by the Modern Movement because (according to them) it didn't *do* anything, except perhaps fall occasionally on passers-by.

Eighteenth-century buildings are stuffed with architectural clichés of this kind, which were still being used right up to the end of the Victorian era, and beyond. Those little pediments over each window, which can be seen in their endless ranks on the façades of Kensington and Earl's Court, came originally from the roofs of Greek temples; and of course by Victoria's day they had become absurdly elaborate for their function, which was only to keep the rainwater away from the windows themselves.

One of the tenets of what one might call the reductionist school of English is that the simpler alternative should always be preferred. Don't say 'To all intents and purposes', Eric Partridge admonishes us. Say 'virtually'. Don't say 'having neither chick nor child'. Say 'childless'. Harry Fieldhouse, in a recent handbook of advice on how to write good English, comes to discuss the word quagmire, a word he seems to dislike. Why not settle, he asks, for 'bog'?[7] There is a perfectly *practical* alternative to those elaborate pediments – a straight hoodmould like the ones on Tudor buildings. But it is not a proper alternative at all, any more than 'bog' is an alternative to 'quagmire'.

Then there were those little dentils and corbels under the cornices, and very pretty and complicated they became. The corbels were supposed to hold up the cornices, but by and by it was the other way round, for they were probably only made of plaster and the cornices were holding up them. They were the architectural equivalent of Eric Partridge's 'fly-blown phrases and metaphors that are now pointless,' but you could say that some of them were already pointless when the ancient Greeks used them, being a throwback (like the mutules of Doric temples) to the days when roofs were made of wood and the rafters stuck out under the eaves. ('We are returning to honesty,' said Gropius. How far back do we have to go?) But European architects several centuries later were still shamelessly delighting their clients with these self-same ideas, till the aesthetics of the Modern Movement required them to put away such toys, in just the same way that modern critical fashion was belabouring the poet Gray for spattering his poems with phrases taken from Pindar and Horace.

'The ground', Pevsner wrote in 1940, 'had first to be cleared of the weeds of nineteenth-century sham ornamentation',[8] – which, translated into a different medium, is what Wordsworth was saying about eighteenth-century poetic diction, and J. H. Badley about the classical curriculum at Rugby, and the revolutionary students of the late 1960s about outmoded cultural values.

Gropius believed in communal utility. The main advantage of the new style – though he was also careful to point out that there was no such thing as a 'Bauhaus style' – was that it allowed ordinary people to lead happier and healthier lives.

> The unification of architectural components would have the salutary effect of imparting that homogeneous character to our towns which is the distinguishing mark of a superior urban culture.[9]

The early work of the Modern Movement was very exciting. It is impossible not to be thrilled by Gropius's vision of light and air as a building's supporting members became more and more tenuous, and walls disappeared or were magically transformed into sheets of glass, whose 'sparkling insubstantiality, and the way it seems to float between wall and wall imponderably as the air, adds a note of gaiety to our modern homes'. So the old idea of a window as a hole knocked through a solid supporting wall could increasingly give place to 'the continuous horizontal casement, subdivided by thin steel mullions, characteristic of the New Architecture'. And there could be endless chains of hanging gardens... Frank Lloyd Wright called it the etherealisation of architecture, and Pevsner described Gropius's and Meyer's Model Factory in Cologne as sublime: 'Never since the Sainte Chapelle and the choir of Beauvais had the human art of building been so triumphant over matter.'[10]

Alas, we know the rest of the story. The casements have lost their magic, the thin steel mullion no longer lifts the heart. They are the common, everyday language of modern institutional and urban building, with no more to say to us than the most perfunctory exchange of platitudes at a conventional dinner-table. It is a desperate reflection – that the search for honesty, purity and truth, so bravely and hopefully undertaken, should have arrived at so feeble an outcome, so monotonous a townscape. The trouble is that, in their efforts to attain purity, the buildings simply end up with what the profession would call insufficient visual content, which means that there is not enough to busy the eye. Having jettisoned all the familiar apparatus of pediments, arches, pilasters, carved spandrels, angel-infested beams, foliated capitals, the honeysuckle, the acanthus, the palm, the plantain, the vine – having shed, as it seemed to him, all this burden, the architect brought up in the Modern Movement has left himself with too meagre a language, too thin a vocabulary, with which to express what he is trying to convey. The whole thing becomes a bore. The effect is most obvious in modern cities, which consist predominantly of large, cellular blocks of flats and offices, giving little opportunity for the exploitation of big spaces, so that it is hardly possible to avoid the almost perpetual repetition of similar mass-produced motifs, spread over larger and larger frontages.

The point was effectively demonstrated by the architect Richard Rogers, an expert witness at the Palumbo inquiry in 1984. Peter Palumbo, the developer, had proposed a splendid new skyscraper opposite the Mansion House in London, said to have been designed by the great modernist Mies van der Rohe, and conservationists had objected. Mr Rogers (I write from hearsay here) declared that the building had Mies's unmistakable stamp, and should therefore be allowed planning permission. On being cross-questioned, and shown details of various buildings in the modern manner, he declined to pick out those designed by Mies. Well, they all looked the same, didn't they?

There must be a limit to Gropius's principle, that 'repetition of the same things for the same purposes exercises a settling and civilising influence on men's minds'. He is right to say it – indeed, its rightness is one of the themes of this book – but it obviously risks the fate of any other generalisation, when too assiduously applied. Go to Sheffield, or Bradford, or East Croydon, and you will see what I mean. (By Ruskin's definition, of course, the buildings to be seen there are not architecture anyway, but let that pass.)

So, again, one set of clichés – the stuccoed fronts with their egg-and-dart mouldings and temple-like porches, the plinth, the shaft, the architrave – has been replaced by another, less rich set of clichés – the concrete mullion, the curtain wall, the steel support in its synthetic marble wrapping: a desolate exchange. It was not what the pioneers wanted. (Nor did the student leaders of 1968, when their own new world was about to dawn, mean to see their successors of five years later engaged in stupefying ideological wrangles.)

The minimalist version of New Movement architecture, a sort of *reductio ad nihil*, can today be found in a minor rash of post-modernist buildings whose outer faces consist entirely of continuous sheets of reflective glass. These sheets are hung indiscriminately over walls and openings alike, and therefore give no clue to the building's structure or to what it is like inside. In this sense a building thus designed is not part of the Modern Movement at all, but rather a betrayal of it. All the glass does is to reflect *other* buildings, from which it borrows a certain interest. (There is a pleasing example in Fetter Lane in London, where the skin of a new office block prettily reflects the mock-Tudor splendours of the rear of the Records Office opposite.) But if all buildings were clothed in reflective glass, then there would obviously be nothing to reflect except more of the same, in the form of other reflective buildings. By analogy, if anyone were to find means of removing all stock phrases from our language, we should end up with the linguistic equivalent of a city of glass buildings, all reflecting each other, which would be more or less meaningless.

After this point the parallel goes wrong, as we knew it would sooner or later. The Bauhaus got many of its ideas from Morris and the Arts and Crafts Movement, in which the great aim had been to supersede the gentleman-artist-architect. Pevsner makes the point that the gentleman-architect tradition stemmed from the Romantics – Schiller, Coleridge, Shelley, Keats – with their belief in a high priesthood of art. But it was this same Romantic tradition, in another of its manifestations, which by not too long a stretch could be said to have led eventually to the individualism encouraged by progressive English teachers since the Second World War. In either case, by different means, a similar position is arrived at – a general repudiation, that is, of traditional forms so as to embrace or create new ones which are supposed to be closer to Real Life, and therefore more democratic. I have tried to suggest how, in the case of architecture, such a bid for new freedoms can bring us unexpectedly into a new form of slavery. As for democracy, who can say that what goes on in an architect's office today is any closer to the *demos*, the people, than it was eighty years ago?[11] Ask the family on the sixteenth floor of the tower block. But I will say no more about that; it has been said before.

3 · 'Are you receiving me?'

What about the case of language? Can we not talk about slavery there too? After all, language can be made to do much beastlier things than architects can do. And since more people are using English now, and at a greater rate – computers can spew words at a speed once thought impossible – it is undoubtedly the vehicle for more deception and self-deception, fraud and humbug than it ever was before.

The 'right' answer is that, in the free world at any rate, the uses of English have become so diverse that it could not possibly lead to anything like slavery. It has a thousand blooms. But diversity carries its own dangers; unless there is a large stock of common references, which are generally understood, communication becomes uncertain. And there is no doubt that, in English, the common stock is diminishing.

The emphasis put on 'relevance' by teachers of English in

schools must carry part of the blame. In their efforts to engage the interest of their pupils, the schools have very naturally preferred to put in front of them those parts of literature which seem of most immediate concern to them and to their own culture, which means Sillitoe rather than Stevenson, Golding rather than Goldsmith; Brontë out, Barstow in; Larkin yes, Langland no. It is not that anyone who *wants* to read Milton or Sheridan or Fanny Burney is prevented from studying any of these. It merely means that the syllabuses are likely more and more readily to relegate them to the status of down-page options. It also means that the pupil who goes for the 'relevant' option, the text which speaks most clearly to his or her own condition, may not be increasing his experience, but only confirming what he already feels; without knowing it, he is denying himself a huge range of ideas. We are back again with the sovereignty of the individual intellect, which at best results in mere impoverishment, and at its worst in a sort of universal self-indulgence, where the highest aim is the pursuit of personal happiness: this above all, to thine own self be true. And how can a man communicate effectively if his most important concern is to listen to what is happening between his own ears?

The hard-pressed teacher, working at what used facetiously to be called the chalk-face, will be unimpressed by all this. He might even have a colloquial word for it. 'Come down for a moment from wherever you are,' he will say, 'and meet my pupils. If they're not going to read Sillitoe they're certainly not going to read Sterne. They probably wouldn't be reading anything at all, apart from the popular newspapers and perhaps the DIY journals or the women's magazines. I don't suppose you've read the Bullock Report?'[1]

The what?

'Lord Bullock's report on literacy. Shows up all the talk in the Tory papers about a decline in standards. See that girl over there? She's doing five CSEs, including English. At her age her grandmother was chopping sticks and blacking the kitchen range. And here you have the, er, excuse me, the cheek to give us this fancy talk about self-indulgence.'

Agreed, agreed. Two worries remain, though. The first is that it would be a very serious matter if our old literary heritage, most of which is still available in paperback, were to be left in the hands of the mandarins. This is precisely the reverse of what was had in mind by those who framed the Education Act of 1944. It is the reverse of what was hoped for by the local authorities which abolished the separatist system and turned all their secondary schools into comprehensives.

The other worry is that if everyone is following his or her own option, each with its particular assumptions and values, reflected in its own range of vocabulary, the common area of understanding will shrink.

The opposite is admittedly depressing. I remember visiting a second-class public school in the West Country many years ago and poking my nose into one of the classroom cupboards. Out fell a pile of books. They were all the same title – La Fontaine's *Fables*, I think, or it may have been *Tartarin de Tarascon* – and all were horribly dog-eared, their fly-leaves a palimpsest of names. That teacher had been taking a whole term, perhaps more, over that one text, for each generation of pupils. Here was thin gruel indeed. (One has the same depressing feeling about the idea of several million people, on a given Thursday morning, all having exactly the same quotations inside their heads, which they have absorbed from a popular television programme, whether on the life of Elgar, or the latest industrial strike, or the doings at Dallas.) I believe it does still happen in schools, and as local education authorities get more and more starved of funds, it may happen more often in the future. Meanwhile most schools would (I suggest) still subscribe to the theory, even if it does not come to much in practice, that a pupil should as far as possible be able to follow his own literary inclinations.

This process – the process whereby the area of shared literary experiences gets gradually smaller – has a nasty tendency to feed on itself. We can see a good example of this when we consider the fate of the Book of Common Prayer. I am not going to raise the well-rehearsed question of whether the Almighty is more likely to listen to a modern vocabulary or to an archaic one; doubtless it is all the same to the Eternal Father. It is not just a question of old versus new; it is also a matter of what the liturgists have been trying to make the new Prayer Book *say*.

The Liturgical Commission which produced the alternatives to the Book of 1662 had two clear aims. The first and most important one had to do with doctrine. They thought that the 1662 version of the Communion Service, for example, put too much stress on sin and not enough on redemption. They wanted to remind the worshipper less of the wrath of God than of His compassion. So the General Confession in the new versions shows far less contrition than the old one did. No longer is the congregation required to say that the memory of its sins is grievous, nor is their burden intolerable. Instead we have something much more like a polite expression of regret.

The second aim was to make sure that everyone in the congregation was in no doubt about what they were hearing or saying. Some of them might indeed understand the ornaments of seventeenth-century prose, but then again others might not. Cranmer had been well aware of the problem and had therefore loaded his liturgy with synonyms or near-synonyms – 'full, perfect and sufficient sacrifice, oblation and satisfaction for the sins of the whole world,' he put, so that those who did not know what oblation meant would at any rate understand 'sacrifice' or 'satisfaction'. The new liturgists took the reductionist way. Thus the splendours of Cranmer's Prayer of Consecration, the heart's centre of the rite, come down to language like this:

Accept our praises heavenly father, through your Son our saviour Jesus Christ; and as we follow his example and obey his command, grant that by the power of your holy spirit these gifts of bread and wine may be to us his body and blood.[2]

(Cranmer: '. . . and grant that we receiving these thy creatures of bread and wine, according to thy Son our saviour Jesus Christ's holy institution, in remembrance of His death and passion, may be partakers of His most blessed body and blood.')

'Accept our praises' – 'follow his example' – these are the phrases of the farewell dinner, the speech of welcome, the secretary's report to the board. But that is the point. They are the language that everyone can understand, or, in current terms, relate to. They are the wretched, minimal residue, all that is left when the excrescences, the peculiarities, have been removed. The Liturgical Commission knew exactly what it was doing. It was adopting the policy of what the architects of the Modern Movement had called common utility, when they decided to do away with the formal excrescences of traditional architecture.

In this particular, the architects had more excuse than the liturgists. The Edwardian baroque had become, shall we say, somewhat overblown. But the liturgists had a difficulty of their own. They wanted to express in the new services something which every member of the congregation would believe in, and there were considerable divergences. So they had to make the priest (or President, in some versions of the new rite) use the words 'may be to us his body and blood', a form entirely colourless and unspecific. Cranmer's Prayer Book, too, had fudged the question of the Real Presence in the bread and wine, but the new liturgy had to fudge it yet further. Now that the Church of England is revealing wider and wider differences of belief, we can expect the language in which it conveys the truths of the Gospel to get closer and closer to that of the communiqué of an international agency, or of a summit meeting. But this is off my subject.

Cranmer's, even in its day, was a ritual language; the Alternative Service Book's is at times not very different from that of a cabled message, economical and without colour. We see the same thing happening in the New English Bible.

> For thou shalt break forth on the right and on the left, and thy seed shall inherit the Gentiles,

says the 1611 version of Isaiah, liv, 3.

> For you shall break out of your confines right and left; your descendants shall dispossess wide regions,

says the New English Bible. Here the aim was somewhat different from that of the Alternative Book: it was a question of accuracy. The result, however, is the same. The Alternative Book is prosaic, and it is meant to be prosaic. There must be no *echoes*. The new liturgists thought that echoes would get in the way of the worship. One member of the Liturgical Commission told me that people who went to the 1662 services might, particularly if they did not go very often, be going for the wrong reasons – for aesthetic reasons, perhaps. The new forms made it clear what it was all really about.

A fresh translation can be very effective. When, in the King James version of the Bible, St Paul asks the people of Colossi to avoid evil concupiscence, a modern congregation, hearing the phrase read out in the Epistle, goes on snoozing. Call it sexual immorality, and some of them might sit up a bit. 'We are returning to honesty of thought and feeling.' Gropius again. But let us look once again where it can lead us; let us see what can happen, not in buildings but in language, when we decide to abandon the supposedly outworn conventions in pursuit of honesty and – whatever the word might mean – truth.

I am thinking particularly of the language of the affections. We all know how extraordinarily difficult it is nowadays to write a letter of condolence. Obituarists have the same difficulty. Paying a compliment in writing, to someone we admire, can be agony. Why?

Because we no longer have the vocabulary. Or rather, we choose not to make use of it. Here is H. S. Holland writing to Mary Gladstone in 1886, condoling with her on the death of Alfred Lyttelton's wife Laura:

> A lovely vision she was – beautiful – like a swift angel, that passes as we look, with a flying glance over the shoulder, at us who must follow whither she draws us . . . You know how she touched a place and people and made us see divinity where formerly had been bricks and mortar and the ordinary jog-trot.[3]

And again, from the same writer:

> Thank you for your letter, full of sweet pathetic memories of that Bird-spirit who lies sleeping so still and silent in The Glen. Poetry wakes up at her touch, and it is hardly possible but that those who remember her will not know a little more of what it is to be felt moving under the great lines, 'O lyric love, half angel and half bird.' The fluttering passion of the *bird* with the white flashing purity of the *angel* – the wonder, the strangeness, the delight of a visitant presence, caught and held in the body for a space, for our joy, and released from restraint to fly back in a rush to the home that was hers all along, leaving to us the sense of swift passage, as of a bird, through a world that could not hold her, so that we are left startled out of our humdrum selves, knowing that we have entertained our angels unawares.

How we shrink from such terms now! Lovely vision, flying glance, sweet memories, fluttering passion: clichés, clichés! Who now, in a letter of condolence, can write of entertaining an angel unawares? We cannot use such phrases, because, not being 'original', they cannot be presumed to be 'sincere'. They were not original when Holland used them either, but we need not suppose that Mr Gladstone's daughter doubted their sincerity. She would not have thought of them as clichés, but as the most telling and most convenient means of conveying a recognisable idea.

So would the recipient of this, from the uncle of the deceased:

> This morning a letter from Edward brought me the sad and melancholy tidings of your dear son Standish's death. From my heart I sincerely condole with you and his afflicted Mother after this heavy and sorrowful trial. Poor dear fellow ... He was, indeed, full of promise and had he lived would have proved a comfort and a solace to your old age ...
> [From the Haly Family papers, 1851)[4]

Now that we have abandoned formal for informal language – the only place where formal language still flourishes is among prime ministers who need to write public expressions of gratitude to Cabinet Ministers whom they have sacked – even the simplest and most direct words and phrases, such as those above, have become difficult for us. In 1781 Hannah More, writing to one of her family about the death of a friend who was an atheist, said: 'He was an honest, good-natured man ... I cannot think of him without horror and compassion.'[5] Well, we certainly can't use the word 'compassion', can we? It has been done, if you will forgive the phrase, to death. But could we even use the expression 'honest and good-natured'? Much too perfunctory, surely? So we search and search for a suitable form of words. 'I was shocked,' one writes, 'to hear of Jane's going.' And probably one was indeed shocked, and at one time the word would have done nicely – earlier letter-writers were always using it – but now it won't do because there is nothing to show that we actually *mean* it. So what shall we say? I was desolated, sad, very sad, so very upset . . . ? We are lost.

Our ancestors were not troubled by the notion that if a person used an expression that had been used before he was therefore not speaking from the heart. But then they had not all been brought up to think that originality was important. Because there was a far larger area of agreed assumptions, it was not then necessary to think up one-off ways of expressing them. For example, at one time every cultivated person had a commonly-held idea of what a 'Christian gentleman' was. (Today the words invite ridicule.) The formal language of eighteenth and nineteenth-century tombstones, in which similar or nearly identical phrases crop up again and again, was able to convey the idea of such a man in unmistakable terms.

> His virtues did honour to human nature. He was generous and charitable without ostentation; of elegant manners, friendly and hospitable, he lived revered and died lamented by all who had the happiness of knowing his worth.

That is what they said of Lord Bateman, of Shobdon, in 1804. It was the ideal of the good squire. And here is another ideal, the perfect wife:

> After having fulfilled for eighteen years the duties of a most affectionate, prudent and pious wife, after having modestly exerted talents and acquirements of no ordinary nature, she died (alas for him who lives to record it) in the 43rd year of her age . . . She departed this life on October 6th, 1853, with the calmness of Christian resignation and in humble reliance on the merits of her redeemer.

That was Susanna Matilda Hodgson, widow of a Herefordshire vicar. In a daughter, other qualities were expected, such as those of Mary Jane, second daughter of Sir George Cornwall,

> who in her seventeenth year was lamentably drowned in the river Wye on the 5th of August 1839. She possessed an active, intelligent and reflective mind, an amiable, frank and cheerful disposition, and was so dearly beloved by her relations and friends, that her sudden removal from them, in the prime of her youth and the fullness of her promise, was the cause of a deep and enduring affliction.

This still transmits its pathos, though the writer of the epitaph did not particularise: he or she could not convey a sense of the *ipsissima persona*, which, like everyone else's, was unique. But we can never do that, so whoever it was did not try. From another inscription we learn that a girl who died at the age of ten was steadfast, cheerful, resigned and reconciled to the will of her Maker, and we would expect no less of her. Other more personal adjectives might be added which might or might not touch a chord in the reader, but they could not restore the image of the child. This does not mean that the generalisations were insincere. Insincerity quickly proclaims itself in such memorials, as in this one of 1831, of another parson:

> Unavailing are the tributes of affection to departed worth, but if sorrow ever claimed a record on the monument of a father, it is here asked for him, who to a rare firmness and steadfastness of principle united a kindness of heart peculiarly his own, who as the promoter of peace and charity among his neighbours diffused the happiness which was centred in his home, and who living and dying manifested his grateful acknowledgment of a superintendent providence and his humble reliance on the mercies of his redeemer.[6]

I am not saying for a moment that the man who penned this particular load of turnips did not care for his father. To identify feeling, or lack of it, in a particular style of prose is admittedly a tricky business. He may have said to himself, 'Goodness how I did love Father, I must do him a really nice epitaph', but, having no taste, was unable to come up with the goods: like those presents children sometimes give, a little lop-sided, not too well painted, but don't they melt the heart? I do not think, however, that the above epitaph comes into this category. The man may have loved his father, but at the time he was actually composing the epitaph he was not thinking of his father at all. He was thinking how clever and literary he was, with his inversions ('Unavailing are . . .' Ugh!) and his way of making an abstract quality, like sorrow, the subject of a sentence. To be fair to him, I don't think he wrote it at all. It was done at his request, by a disinterested friend.

Whoever wrote it, we just *know* that H. S. Holland's tribute to Laura Lyttelton, which is equally mannered, is more genuine than this. (Strangely enough, it goes off the rails in just the same way as the other, by personification: 'Poetry wakes up at her touch . . .') Certainly the Georgians could get it wrong too. Equally certainly the Victorians had too sweet a tooth for our taste. But neither they nor the Georgians were embarrassed, as we are, by these occasions.

It was not the elaboration of their language which mainly distinguishes them from us. It was their ability to use a word or phrase with the certainty that it would be taken at its face value. The same thing can be seen in the matter of compliments. When in May, 1829, David Wilkie writes to Sir Thomas Lawrence, who has publicly praised him in a presidential address to the Royal Academy,

> Permit me, then, my dear Sir, most humbly to thank you for this mark of your kindness, feeling as I do in the absence of all claim that in receiving it from one [so] great and

> distinguished as you are, I feel that I am most honoured in being allowed to call it kindness,[7]

he risks being thought of as a toady – and he probably was one, a bit. *We* could not manage any such thing at all, in a similar situation. ('Mark of your kindness'? – 'great and distinguished'? The man must be joking. Get me out of here.) The thing was, that he was able to say it, this very difficult thing, *and* to show, in a few words, why it was difficult. And here is Ruskin, expressing his friendship for Dr John Brown the Scottish medico:

> Yes, indeed, I shall always regard you as one of the truest, fondest, faithfullest friends I have.[8]

Try that on your chums. And who could now say this of a dying sister, as Edward Lear, writing to Lord Carlingford in 1861, did of his sister Ann?

> Poor dear creature, her sufferings are very sad, yet she is *absolutely* cheerful and tranquil, & speaks of dying as a change about to bring such great delight that she only checks herself for thinking of it too much. She has always been indeed as near to Heaven as it was possible to be.[9]

Nowadays we cannot be absolutely certain that the person we are writing to believes in Heaven; we may not do so ourselves; so there's another landmark gone, by which to steer our feelings. We almost envy the writer of another letter from the Haly papers, this time about the death of her father in 1835:

> I needs must tell you what a dreadful blow it has been to us all. It has indeed pleased God to lay his heaviest hand upon us, but God's will be done – and it is not for us to question his decree ... [My father], poor soul, was quite resigned,

indeed his last most wonderful strength of mind and composure during that whole week of intense suffering astonished all those about him ... I do wish you could have seen the happy countenance and sweet smile of your dear father who had suffered so much ... indeed it had quite the effect of composing us, and we have felt that there was something inevitably drawing us back into the house and have felt how selfish it would be of us to wish him back in this world of sorrow.

It is well said and deeply felt, though there was nothing unusual or startling about the writer's sentiments. For her, as for Edward Lear, there was the certainty of eternity.

Actually Lear's general instincts seem to have been no different, in the matter of condolences, from ours today. Writing to Lady Waldegrave about the death of her husband George Harcourt, he includes all the natural sentiments we generally have – the shock of the news, how much longer the deceased might have lived, premonitions of his death, how bereft his correspondent must feel, how comforting her memories of her husband must be, and so forth. It is because they are so commonplace that we find them hard. Lear evidently did not find them so (though we discover him a few days later writing to Carlingford: 'I am *much pleased* that Lady W. liked my letter'). See how he manages it:

> ... And it appears to me that this sudden breaking of a close tie must have affected you particularly:– for in spite of the difference in age & of your natural dispositions, death, after a union of many years, must assuredly keenly affect the survivor of the two, when, as I know to be the case with yours, the nature of the one is left full of warmth & truth.[10]

No wonder Lady W. liked the letter. Would not a widow, today, be delighted with such a letter? She probably would – but she probably wouldn't get one, because the latter-day Lear would be scared stiff lest he commit a cliché, and he would almost certainly class 'keenly affect' and 'warmth and truth' as clichés, or polite nothings.

That same Dr Brown, whom I have mentioned as Ruskin's friend, wrote in 1866 to his aunt Molteno, whom he had neglected by not answering her earlier letters:

> My dearest Aunt – Your kind letter of this morning made my cheeks glow with shame.[11]

An apologetic nephew could not say that now, if he wanted to show that he was truly sorry (and it is evident from the context that Dr Brown *was* sorry); he could not use the words, unless he did not really mean them.

Any educated person like Dr Brown, who felt very deeply about something or someone, and found his own tongue inadequate, had a further resource in Latin, with its enormous evocations. Writing to Lady Trevelyan about his lately-dead wife (who, to judge from the bust of her by William Brodie, must have been a honey), he says this:

> I am fuller of her and her faithfulness and loveliness and dearness than I was months ago. I am republishing *Locke and Sydenham* [a paper he had read to the Harveian Society about Locke's medical studies]; it has been much asked for, and she always liked it best, and encouraged me to write it; and I have a sort of silly wish to put her name into it, but very likely I shall not. I thought of something like this: *Patronae meae et uxori – Tibi, Catherina mea! Pulchra, pia, semper carissima, evanesca donec aspiret dies et fugiant umbrae* . . .[12]

Brown was not a pretentious man, though he could be twee (he addressed Catherine as 'my dear little wifikie'). There was nothing forced about his lapidary outburst. For both he and

Lady Trevelyan had at their disposal not only the stock of formal English, but also this marvellous reserve tank, as it were. *Pia*, by the way, did not mean just 'pious', a word which in English has come sadly down in the world: it implied a now untranslatable loyalty to ancestors, family and friends, and carried with it a fragment of the huge tapestry of the *Aeneid*.

We have thrown all that away too, of course.

In short, in our efforts to be different, to cast off the dead paraphernalia of the past – to stand, as it were, in our own shoes – we find ourselves strangely naked. We have congratulated ourselves on our freedom, and have ended up tongue-tied.

Let me make it clear that I am not suggesting that the English language is falling into a state of decay, or anything like that. It is, in fact, flourishing. As I have said, it can be found in more exotic forms, in more luxuriant outgrowths, than ever. And there is still some good journalism, even in the *Times*. The serious novel is still being written, partly because novelists have discovered areas of experience which were formerly taboo, partly because they have been able to make use of a whole new corpus of knowledge provided by the psychological sciences, partly because there are new social conventions to record – oh, for a hundred reasons. I am not concerned with them here. I am concerned with what one might call everyday speech and writing, not with special effects. It may well be objected that the letters and epitaphs from which I have quoted above were pretty special themselves, in the sense that their authors had their own ways of putting things, and that we have simply decided not to express ourselves like that any more. But – and this is the point – *we have nothing to put in their place.*

4 · 'Camp' clichés

This does not mean that we no longer use clichés. Of course we do. They can be classified in two different ways. First, there is a clear distinction to be made between those that are written and those that are spoken. Second, does the speaker or writer, as the case may be, *know* that he or she is perpetrating a cliché? Is he doing it because it comes naturally to him in any case – because he has that sort of not very original mind – or is he doing it on purpose?

The two classifications overlap considerably. I will resist the temptation to draw one of those tiresome Venn diagrams with shaded or dotted areas, much loved by a certain sort of lecturer, who thinks that if he has found the right category for something he has mysteriously explained what it actually is. And I refuse to provide a visual analysis like those used to explain institutional structures, infested with boxes, arrows and similar apparati, so often a substitute for thought.

Among the on-purpose variety, there is a vast artillery of what one might call 'camp' clichés, which are in constant use. The word 'camp' has several different meanings and is not very satisfactory, but as I have been unable to find another, it will have to do. The 1972 Supplement to the Oxford English Dictionary has 'ostentatious, exaggerated, affected, theatrical' (also 'effeminate or homosexual', which is not what I have in mind here) and gives a nice example from Cecil Beaton dating from 1954: 'Naval commanders or jolly colonels acquired the *camp* manners of calling everyone from Joan of Arc to Merlin "lots of fun", and the adjective "terrible" peppered every sentence.' In other words the commanders and the colonels were not really being themselves; they were being affected and theatrical, which is what I mainly think of when I talk about a cliché being 'camp'.

In this category comes the rueful phrase, usually but by no means always the spoken phrase, of which the speaker is perfectly well aware that it is a chestnut and that it will be recognised as one, but tacitly admits that it is the best he can think of. Many people cannot do without them. They seem to say: 'I know very well that this is a stock phrase, but, if you will forgive me, it's the only one that truly defines the feeling I'm trying to convey. A less sophisticated writer would probably put inverted commas round it. Anyway, I hope you will detect the shrug of the shoulders with which I offer it to you.'

The speaker (if it is a speaker) may be absolutely serious, he may even be, as he puts it, 'deeply moved', but, for reasons discussed in the last chapter, he can find no other way of expressing his emotion.

'I will strain every nerve,' says the man on the telephone, as he promises whoever it is at the other end that he means to keep a rendezvous. And he really does mean it. Both he and his listener know that this is a tired old phrase, but never mind, it has served its purpose. The person at the other end does not say to himself: 'Ah, my friend has used a dead phrase that has lost its force, therefore I will not believe him, for a man who uses a dead phrase like that is plainly not going to turn up at the agreed hour.' The phrase works, and the appointment is kept, because both the interlocutors understand exactly the weight that should be given to it: it is jokey, not quite facetious; it is a perfectly adequate expression of a serious intention, and it is used precisely because the speaker is reluctant, for fear of being pompous, to put his seriousness in other than a 'camp' manner. He is being no less earnest than, for example, the girl who tells her lover, as his train draws away from the platform, that he must take care, and not do anything rash, and keep off the booze, and other ridiculously trite, commonplace things which mean practically nothing in themselves – she knows, for heaven's sake, that he's not going to get drunk – but really mean 'I love you and I will miss you.' But the wretched girl can't say that, so she has to resort to a quasi-ironical turn of phrase; she is being affected; but again, never mind, because her friend knows exactly what she means. He does not say: 'Ah, she has used a ridiculously trite remark, therefore she does not love me.' He says: 'Ah, she loves me after all.'

Not only are such conventional circumlocutions quite clearly understood by those who use them; one could also say that without them a very large number of people would hardly be able to communicate their feelings. All such devices come under the definition of 'camp' in the sense that the speaker is using a different mode from the one which really suits his meaning – in the case of the man on the telephone, a grander mode, in the case of the girl a more prosaic one.

A man with a splendid ear for the spoken cliché is Keith Waterhouse. In his novel *Office Life*[1] he has well caught the kind of self-protective devices used by middle-class clerks, the Pooters of the 1970s and 1980s, when they talk at work. The hero, Gryce, arriving at a new billet, is asked, not 'Why did you leave your last job?' but 'What prompted you to transfer your allegiance?' He explains how he had 'for my sins, served before the mast for three years with So-and-So's.' One clerk asking for an order-book says to another: 'Have you finished with the book of words, Amanda, light of my heart?' A colleague wanting to look at the staff holiday rota says: 'Let us consult the holy writ.' Gryce makes friends by showing he knows the right phrases, calling the coffee-vendor 'an infernal machine' and the coffee 'a witches' brew.'

It is beautifully done. We may note the *literary* flavour of it all, so different from the circumlocutions of the saloon bar, which have their own language. Mr Waterhouse's hero, liking the smell of a canteen dish, says: 'I was enticed by the tempting aroma of the shepherd's pie'; his characters don't say 'Really, honestly', but 'Rest assured.'

Phrases like this began their careers in respectable company and have gradually gone downhill; like Black Beauty, born a thoroughbred, finding himself in livery stables, and eventually working as a broken-down cabhorse, they hobnob with the great writers, get tired, do a long spell in national newspapers, are relegated to the provinces, and end up, working as hard as ever, as poor old camp clichés in the offices of London export firms. Unlike Black Beauty, they will not be rescued, but there is life in them yet.

Happily, there are plenty of stock phrases still being put to very good use on their way to the knacker's yard. Bernard Levin, for example, has a fine stableful of them, and he has a sure eye for the best one to take out for exercise on a given occasion. Here he is poking fun at Lady Caroline Blackwood, who had rather overdone her distaste at the sight of some American airmen, at their missile base at Greenham Common, baring their bottoms at her. 'The world', wrote Mr Levin,

> is full of wars and rumours of wars; famine, pestilence and sudden death are not yet eradicated; the heart of man still contains an ample store of envy, hatred, malice and all uncharitableness . . . Here, milady, is a leper; over there, an

orphan child weeps ... Still shocked, still appalled, still never seen anything so unpleasant? Go to, you great ninny ...[2]

For indignation over the larger-scale miseries, those Biblical echoes still make their point; Mr Levin could hardly have made it so well himself; in the borrowed phrases he has found the perfect shorthand. Here they are serious, and yet not entirely so, for there is a suggestion of satire in them: the writer is, after all, ridiculing someone. I doubt if they could be used in earnest, that is to say, in other than a satirical or polemical way. At any rate, they work.

One fears that there will come a time when they no longer do so, because the literature from which they are taken will be unfamiliar to most readers of *The Times*. 'Wars and rumours of wars' has already disappeared from Matthew xxiv 6 in the *New English Bible* version. Now it's 'The noise of battle near at hand and the news of battles far away', which is unlikely to acquire the status of a cliché, or be used by anyone for the purposes of evocation. And there is no 'uncharitableness' in the Alternative Service Book's revision of the Litany.

It has not happened yet; and it could be argued — indeed, I have heard it argued — that when it does, such phrases will *ipso facto* cease to be clichés in any proper sense, as they will come fresh to the eye. 'Don't worry,' said a very experienced journalist to whom I put the problem. 'You pick out a phrase from the storehouse, and think it will strike a chord. Well, if they don't recognise it, they'll think you invented it yourself, and you'll get the credit, so you can't lose.' It sounded a comforting idea, but it will not really do; the echoes produced by writers like Bernard Levin, whose work is purposely mannered, depend for their effect on the recognition of the source, or at least on the *frisson* the reader gets from knowing that, somewhere, he has heard or read that before.

The pleasure of recognition, as we all know, goes deep.

Keith Waterhouse's office clerks get tremendous satisfaction from recognising each other's clichés. Half such pleasure comes simply from the knowledge that everyone is speaking the same language. It is a code. I am told that spiders have such codes, though theirs are visual rather than verbal: *Lycosa lugubris* stretches his front legs sideways and raises alternate palps; *Euophrys frontalis* waves his legs up and down; *Ballus* adopts a nautical roll.[3] Each knows that unless he does this, his mate will fail to recognise him as one of her own species, and he will get eaten up. So office talk, or any talk among people getting to know each other, is self-protective in two ways: it signals your species, and it offers a sort of perpetual mutual reassurance.

It is undoubtedly this pleasure of recognition, this constant return to the familiar, which largely accounts for the universal delight in clichés, despite the obloquy directed at them, first by teachers, then by the supposedly wise and knowing in our adult lives. The received wisdom is that the person who gets caught in possession of a cliché is a pretty bad hat. The *O.E.D.* Supplement (1972) quotes one of Nicholas Blake's characters in his crime novel *Minute for Murder* as saying of another: 'I'll do in the little cliché-monger.' Oh yes, it's an insult all right. From the same source we have 'Television will continue to be clichéd, formula-ridden and bland' (from the *New Left Review*, 1942); and the *Listener* of 30 July 1959, also quoted in the Supplement, has a reference to 'the kind of fond reminiscence which comes rather too near the cliché view of human situations'. They make it sound like an infectious disease. The *Listener* quotation is of particular interest, and I shall be returning to it later.

But, as I say, the cliché will always flourish in one form or another. We need it.

One of the greatest connoisseurs of the cliché was S. J. Perelman, who for many years delighted readers of the *New Yorker*. He had a marvellous feeling for its many literary forms, and brilliantly sent up John Buchan, the Hollywood gossip mags, early twentieth-century euphuists such as Ronald Firbank and all sorts of others. Here, in 'Nesselrode to Jeopardy', he gives us a taste of the sub-Buchan school:

> His harsh voice stabbed at me, insistent as the cicadas in the Mediterranean twilight . . . I heard the sharp, sudden intake of his breath, followed by a little click as he expelled it. When he spoke again, it was in a tight, strangled whisper that put shudders up my spine . . .

And again:

> Yet some sixth sense told me that Reutschler, his hawk's profile taut in the darkness, was close to the answer.[4]

In fact Perelman just adored clichés, and we fully share his pleasure. In his *New Yorker* piece, 'Up the Close and Down the Stair', for example, he uses them not for any particular satirical purpose, but just for the hell of it. As he tries to settle down in his flat in an otherwise deserted brownstone,

> [the telephone] gave a sudden, nerve-shattering peal. I sprang out and flattened myself against the wall near the instrument, every faculty tensed . . . Trying to envision the face at the other end, the twisted smile and the narrow, baleful eyes, I felt perspiration ooze from my scalp.[5]

The man simply can't help it: he has reached the point at which he can tell a story *only* by means of the camp cliché. And perhaps for readers of the *New Yorker*, the story of a man in a spooky, deserted house is best told in just this way. (The Chandleresque technique for similar situations, often involving the casual mention of an unlocatable dripping faucet, has become the source of its own sort of cliché, as used by film directors.)

Like Jerome K. Jerome, Perelman makes effortless use of bathos. In fact he is doing it all the time. 'Ever the thrall of a pair of saucy blue eyes, I good-naturedly complied and sprang down with a graceful bound, sustaining a trifling fracture of the spleen.' (From *Westward Ha!*)[6] 'There was a short dynamic silence, shattered at last by the entrance of our host, Dorian, his arms piled high with Toulouse-Lautrecs. He bore them with athletic ease, possibly because only six years ago he had similarly borne shoulders of mutton in a Chicago slaughterhouse.' (From the same.)[7]

Much earlier than Perelman, Jerome was a master of the camp cliché, as in this passage, from *The Idle Thoughts of an Idle Fellow*, on 'Being Shy':

> [The not-shy man] looks around, and everywhere sees roguish eyes and laughing lips. What more natural than that amidst so many roguish eyes and laughing lips he should become confused, and, forgetting which particular pair of roguish eyes and laughing lips it is that he belongs to, go off making love to the wrong set?[8]

There he is positively taking a cliché by its scruff and exposing it to heavy ridicule. His use of bathos has the same effect – for example, in his passage on rats, which

> scream in shrill, unearthly notes in the dead of night, while the moaning wind sweeps, sobbing, round the ruined turret towers, and passes wailing like a woman through the chamber bare and tenantless.
>
> And dying prisoners in their loathsome dungeons see, through the horrid gloom, their small red eyes like glittering coals ... I love to read about rats. They make my flesh creep so.[9]

It is pure kitsch (*O.E.D.*: sentimentally vulgar). But one suspects that Jerome did not always quite know what mode he was writing in. As Perelman did later, he got taken over, as it were. Some of his riper paragraphs might seem (since he was, after all, a comic) to be obvious camp, but on second glance one wonders. There is no irony in the following, despite the promise of the first six words:

> And autumn! Ah, how sadly fair, with its golden glow, and the dying grandeur of its tinted woods – its blood-red sunsets, and its ghostly evening mists, with its busy murmur of reapers, and its laden orchards, and the calling of the gleaners, and the festival of praise![10]

One waits for the squelch-line, but it never comes. When Jerome writes: 'We see but dimly through the mists that roll around our time-girt isle of life, and only hear the distant surging of the great sea beyond', we can be pretty sure that he is being serious, that he means it.[11] At any rate his public loved him; by 1890 *The Idle Thoughts of an Idle Fellow* had gone, according to its publisher, the Leadenhall Press, into its 137th edition. Nor can Jerome be dismissed as a tosh-merchant. He wrote in desperation for money, but he was too self-aware to be classed as tosh. His great gift was this admirable ability to mix the straight with the camp, sometimes in the same essay, and get away with it. His readers enjoyed it in either case.

That defunct art form, the *Times* Fourth Leader, owed a lot to Jerome. It was still going strong twenty-five years after Jerome's death. A leader of 1953, lamenting the reputation of G. A. Henty, the Victorian writer of stories for boys, expresses itself thus:

> It is truly dreadful to contemplate such profanity and yet it is all too possible: devouring Time has by now made a meal on all those beautiful red and green covers, covered with gold

flourishes, once our pride and joy. Elder persons, however, may shed a tear for that friend of their boyhood and deem the memorial well deserved.

Here we have at least three different classes of cliché in one short passage, a splendid effort: one classical tag, three facetious circumlocutions and a couplet, 'pride and joy'. And does not the word 'deem' set the sentence firmly in its genre? The tone of the Fourth Leader assumes that its reader is an upper-class male; once had a governess and slept in a night-nursery; plays or played a great many games; and remembers some Latin (*Tempus edax*, etc.) from the public school to which he now sends his own son. Bores are 'thundering' and a strain on the strongest character tends to be 'well-nigh intolerable'. Today we find it all rather intolerable ourselves, but in fact it is deftly managed; the old chestnuts are cleverly kept in the air; and there are those deliberate lapses into informality such as had also been part of the stock-in-trade of Jerome. A leader on spaghetti says: 'Regular consumers acquire a remarkable dexterity.' But then: 'Gathering the stuff requires a degree of concentration detrimental to conversation.' The expression 'the stuff' makes us forget the writer is a windbag and turns him into a friendly old buffer.

The Fourth Leaders were popular and at one time appeared in hard-cover collections. In our own day *The Times* has continued to attempt (though with no sure touch) the circumlocutionary cliché, but the proportion of its readers who fall into the category once addressed by its Fourth Leaders must be small indeed. They did, after all, require a certain level of education. In any case, the taste for them is gone.

But the man who brought the art of manipulating the cliché to its very highest level in recent times – indeed, I can think of no one else to touch him – was, of course, P. G. Wodehouse, and he is as popular as ever. He shares with Perelman a delight in the whole business and is believed to have kept always by his side, while he was writing, a reliable dictionary of quotations.[12] Again like Perelman, it is as though he could tell a story only by the ironic use of cliché; and of course the more readily we recognise his plunderings, the greater our own pleasure. He could raid the treasury, and deploy it, with a surer touch than anyone. His technique appears not to have greatly altered from first to last, though he got better at it.

He has been criticised adversely for his perfunctory descriptions of pretty girls; it is undeniable, however, that the girls he describes are as pretty as one could wish for. Here, in *The Reverent Wooing of Archibald*, is a deliberate use of the corniest phrases, openly acknowledged as such, to bring to life a certain type of girl. Mr Mulliner speaking:

> I chanced . . . the other day to pick up a copy of one of the old yellowback novels of fifty years ago . . . It was entitled *Sir Ralph's Secret*, and its heroine, the Lady Elaine, was described as a superbly handsome girl, divinely tall, with a noble figure, the arched Montresor nose, haughty eyes beneath delicately pencilled brows, and that indefinable air of aristocratic aloofness which marks the daughter of a hundred earls. And Aurelia Cammarleigh might have been this formidable creature's double.[13]

Every phrase is straight from stock. Incidentally, Mr Mulliner says that the book *Sir Ralph's Secret* belonged to 'Miss Postlethwaite, our courteous and erudite barmaid', with the implication that 'the old yellowback novels of fifty years ago' were still being read by working-class girls in 1929, though one must admit that Wodehouse's grasp of such matters was not too firm. Later in the same story the said Aurelia Cammarleigh describes herself as 'rather an outsize and modelled on the lines of Cleopatra',[14] an archetype he was to use again in 1966 for his description of the formidable Lady

Constance, Lord Emsworth's sister, 'a forceful and imperious woman modelled on the lines of the late Cleopatra.'[15]

The convention in the Mulliner stories is that they are all spoken. Mr Mulliner might be thought of as the sort of cove to whom certain turns of phrase, which would hardly do in print, come naturally *viva voce*. Likewise when Wodehouse quotes Freddie Threepwood's Uncle Galahad, in *Sticky Wicket at Blandings*,[16] as saying,

> I've been giving it intense thought, turning here a stone, exploring there an avenue,

the fact that the sentence is spoken calls for a different attitude towards it from that which we apply to the written word. Our ears are more lenient in these matters than our eyes. Actually in *Sticky Wicket* Wodehouse does not bother much with the distinction. It is written in his own person – there is no 'I' in the story – and it begins:

> It was a beautiful afternoon. The sky was blue, the sun yellow, butterflies flitted, birds tooted, bees buzzed and, to cut a long story short, all Nature smiled. But on Lord Emsworth's younger son Freddie Threepwood . . . these excellent weather conditions made little impression. He was thinking of dog biscuits.

The vocabulary is that of a member of the Drones Club; the real difference is that while the man in the club, or at the bar, may be talking automatically and unselfconsciously, Wodehouse knows that he is using stock phrases and knows that the reader knows too. His sense of rhythm is faultless.

With Mr Mulliner Wodehouse allowed himself a more quaintly old-fashioned, more mannered style than that, better suited to a man of Mulliner's years. Since his stories are all told in the bar of the Angler's Rest, they might theoretically be classed as Pub Cliché (see below, p. 117), but they are really quite different.

Wodehouse puts his description – this time not of a girl but of scenery – in quotes again in 'Sleepy Time' (1966), just as he had in the 1929 story:

> On the subject of Paradise Valley the public relations representative of the Paradise Valley Hotel had expressed himself very frankly. It is, he says in his illustrated booklet, a dream world of breathtaking beauty, and its noble scenery, its soft mountain breezes and its sun-drenched pleasances impart to the jaded city worker a new vim and vigour and fill him so full of red corpuscles that before a day has elapsed in these delightful surroundings he is conscious of a *je ne sais quoi* and a *bien être* and goes about with his chin up and both feet on the ground, feeling as if he had just come back from the cleaner's.[17]

Satire, parody? Not really. Just P.G.'s way of telling the story. Much of his prose is in what one might call invisible quotation marks, as in this piece of nature study in *Unpleasantness at Bludleigh Court*:

> They sat together on a rustic bench overlooking the water. It was a lovely morning. The sun shone on the little wavelets which the dying breeze drove gently to the shore. A dreamy stillness had fallen on the world, broken only by the distant sound of Sir Alexander Bassington murdering magpies...[18]

(Bathos again.) Wodehouse's commonest ploy, however – or at any rate his most often noticed ploy – is the use of literary gobbets, which have given him the mistaken reputation of being an egghead disguised as a lowbrow, though his brow was self-confessedly low. In the Cammarleigh story he quotes an undigested verse from *Maud* – the aim is to give an idea of Archibald's feelings when he hears la Cammarleigh's footstep on the balcony outside his bedroom – but he is generally more subtle. A couple of paragraphs later he describes Archibald's imitation of a hen laying an egg as 'less violent than Salvini's *Othello*' but with 'something of the poignant wistfulness of Mrs Siddons in the sleepwalking scene of *Macbeth*'.

This, as I have said, is Mr Mulliner's voice; elsewhere, as in *Laughing Gas* (1936) he gives the story to a Drone, in this case the newly-ennobled Lord Havershot, whose simple mind could hardly be expected to retain bits of Tennyson. Jeeves and Bertie, the best-loved Drone of them all, were the perfect partnership and the perfect vehicle for Wodehouse's pleasure in pat quotations, with Bertie fumbling for the lines and Jeeves supplying the answers.

> *Bertie*: What's that gag of yours? Something about wheels.
> *Jeeves*: Less than the dust beneath thy chariot wheels, sir.[19]

Bertie again, from the same tale:

> I remember Jeeves speaking of someone who was fit for treasons, stratagems and spoils, and that was Bingley all over.

Bertie to Jeeves, later in the book:

> You may leave us, Jeeves. Much obliged for your Daniel coming to judgmenting.

Bertie knew about that, of course, without prompting from Jeeves. Hadn't he won a Scripture prize at school?

One can understand Wodehouse's *tendre* for butlers, those champions of the correct circumlocution for practically everything.

'Camp' clichés

Jeeves: Mr Wooster will bear me out when I say that his lordship was frequently extremely depressed at the thought that he was doing so little to help.
Bertie: Absolutely, by Jove! Quite pipped about it.[20]

What a team!

We need not argue whether Wodehouse used clichés. He chose the phrases that he chose because they *were* clichés, and instantly recognisable as such; but instead of making us groan with boredom they make us laugh, and admire them for being so apt. It is no good suggesting that, since they plainly come outside the definition of a cliché as a phrase or word that has lost its force, they should therefore not be defined as clichés at all, but as something else (what?). The pleasure which so many of us get from reading Wodehouse only demonstrates the dreadful confusion we get ourselves into if we try to label some bits of language as cliché-equals-bad and others as not-cliché-equals-good.

5 · Play it again, Sam

But perhaps we ought to try for a fresh definition? 'A dead phrase that has lost its force' is hardly right for those I have been quoting, though we still call them clichés. So long as a phrase still produces a response in the listener or reader at whom it is directed, it cannot, in the terms of our definition, be properly labelled a cliché, surely?

Perhaps, better still, we ought to abandon the attempt; all we can really do is to talk about different *kinds* of cliché. What are they trying to do, why are they being used, at whom are they directed – and, as I say, does the person directing them know that they are clichés anyway? The difficulty about the expression 'lost its force' is that it has an open end.

Randolph Quirk helps us again here. 'It is not usually a question,' he points out, 'of whether a given expression *out of context* [his italics] is or is not a cliché.'[1] It depends on the occasion. He gives as an example the remark: 'I admired Pinter's incredible insight in that act.' Perfectly all right when said in the foyer. (Well, fairly all right. Professor Quirk is a charitable man.) But certainly not right at all in a review in next morning's paper. Quirk then produces a nice collection of woolly phrases from students' essays, of which he must have had quite a lot of experience at University College, London. For example:

His verse is packed with special meaning.
His poems have a character of their own.
He paints the very body and soul of industrial life.
and, rather more fancy:
His decorative imagery always follows a structural line.

The students who wrote these unhelpful sentences may have had more than one reason. One guesses that they were parroting a bit of what someone else had said. Or they knew they knew nothing about the subject, but, like an inadequately-briefed Cabinet Minister at Question Time, hoped no one would notice. Or they were rather stupid after all, and had not given any thought to the matter. Or the writers did know the subject, but lacked the words to get that knowledge down, and were simply inarticulate. This is the least likely explanation. At any rate no one could possibly say that, in their own context, to use Quirk's expression, these were not clichés.

But what about that enormous category, romantic fiction? What about those who ride the tosh-horse, in Rebecca West's much-used phrase? Such writers are read in their hundreds of thousands. You and I, discriminating creatures that we are, call them cliché-ridden. But do they not, in *their* context, strike a chord? Of course they do, or they would not sell so well.

Tosh is of great interest, because there are so many varieties of it, so many different levels. A. C. Benson, the much-loved and much-respected Master of Magdalene College who wrote the words for 'Land of Hope and Glory', could produce some very fine tosh, and was almost certainly ashamed of it. Like

Jerome K. Jerome, he appealed to the apparently bottomless capacity of his age for pure, straight sentiment. Here, from a series of pieces he wrote in 1905 for the *Cornhill Magazine* under the title *From A College Window*, is a splendid bit of tishery-toshery:

> ... So I sit, while the clock on the mantelpiece ticks out the pleasant minutes, and the fire winks and crumbles on the hearth, till the old gyp comes tapping at the door to learn my intentions for the evening; and then, again, I pass out into the court, the lighted windows of the Hall gleam with the ancient armorial glass, from staircase after staircase come troops of alert, gowned figures, while overhead, above all the pleasant stir and murmur of life, hang in the dark sky the unchanging stars ...[2]

David Newsome, Benson's biographer (who spotted this jewel), comments on the *Cornhill* and other performances:

> The prose becomes urbane and prim, deteriorating, as the books multiply, into cliché ... Gardens are 'peaceful ... with smiling lawns'; trees 'rustle'; pigeons 'roo-hoo' ...[3]

But Benson was cliché-ridden from the start: the clock, the fire, the *old* (of course) college servant, the stained glass – all are reach-me-down images. It is not surprising to learn that *From a College Window* was being parodied in the *Cambridge Review* as early as 1905.

But again, Benson's work was a huge success. His *College Window* alone brought him £600 in royalties in roughly eighteen months, Newsome tells us – a sum which, it will be remembered, was regarded by E. M. Forster in 1910 as being enough to keep either of the Schlegel sisters in comfortable independence for a year.[4]

There is a paradox about this writing of Benson's. For what

he describes in the passage quoted above, however trite it may have seemed to many, was also actually true: it *was* a fair description of the sort of life led by comfortable dons in Edwardian colleges, though the gyp may not always have been as old, nor the gowned figures as alert. Yet to the thousands who read it and clamoured for more of it, it was entirely unreal, and one suspects that they read it for exactly that reason: not because it was true to life, but because, so far as they were concerned, it was precisely the opposite. (Another demonstration of the general proposition, that it is impossible to define a cliché.)

Again, Benson perfectly accurately describes all the noises heard when the eights are out on the river – the 'shrill cries' of the coxes, the 'plash of oars' and the rattly noise of chains being pulled through iron rings. It had a double charm. Old men in pink caps remembered idle undergraduate days, while the readers who had never had them were transported. It scores on familiarity *and* strangeness. It is still high-class tosh, though. And so is this:

> I was visited, as I sate in my room today, by one of those sudden impressions of rare beauty that come and go like flashes, and which leave one desiring a similar experience. The materials of the impression were simple and familiar enough. My room looks out into a little court; there is a plot of grass, and to the right of it an old stone-built wall, close against which stands a row of aged lime-trees. Straight opposite, at right-angles to the wall, is the east side of the Hall, with its big plain traceried window enlivened with a few heraldic shields of stained glass. While I was looking out today there came a flying burst of sun, and the little garden became a sudden feast of delicate colour; the rich green of the grass, the foliage of the lime-trees, their brown wrinkled stems, the pale moss of the wall, the bright points of colour in the emblazonries of the window, made a sudden delicate

harmony of tints. I had seen the place a hundred times before without ever guessing what a perfect picture it made.[5]

Benson then goes into a rumination of the nature of beauty ('The vision of a spring copse with all its tapestry of flowers, bright points of radiant colour, fills us with a strange yearning' etc.). It ought to have been all right. The scene in the 'little court' is closely observed – it is not one of those thoughtless generalisations, without content, which we associate with the tosh-merchant. And it was a genuine experience: we have surely all had one like it. So what is wrong? I knew it was wrong when I first read it, and could not think exactly why. But of course! It is much too pat, the whole box of tricks. 'A sudden delicate harmony of tints' – such a phrase turns a spiritual experience into an amateur water-colour. It reminds one of that excellent poem by Rupert Brooke, called *The Voice*, in which the poet, 'safe in the magic of my woods', is joined by a friend. 'You came and quacked beside me in the wood . . . You said: "The sunset's pretty, isn't it?"'

Poor Benson. He could do better than that. Hugh Walpole was another who, like Benson, wrote too much. After a time he plainly got tired of describing the cathedral town in which a number of his novels are set, and he became more and more perfunctory, as in this fragment from *The Inquisitor*:

> You have never seen it [this is the Bishop writing to an old friend] on a market day when the farmers slap the rumps of the cattle, and the boys finger the volumes on the tuppenny bookstall and in the shadows of the arcades buy toffee-balls for their girls! When, in the spring, you can see through a break in the old grey houses the daffodils blowing on the high banks of the sloping fields, and in the summer roses scent the very provision shops, and in the deep shadow of the High Street the Cathedral bells linger like birds skimming a mountain tarn. And days when . . . you can . . . look down on

the huddle of roofs resting under the evening chimney-smoke and watch the Cathedral towers catch the last triumphant gestures of the setting sun![6]

Again, the objection we must have to this effort is not that it is untrue to life. Walpole is said to have based his cathedral town on Truro, which he knew and loved. I dare say the farmers did slap their cattle's rumps, and assuredly the houses were old and grey. But now we simply do not believe it. Why not? Because those daffodils, those roses, are straight off the shelf. And the bells are, I suppose, more or less compulsory. It is all a great pity, for Walpole could be a fine writer. We cannot excuse him on the ground that he has put this tuppence-coloured description into the mouth, or rather pen, of a sentimental old bishop (one is glad to have been spared his sermons). Walpole is out of fashion now, but in his day he was very popular indeed. It is worth adding that he himself had a great deal to say about the truth – the realism, as he called it – of his novels, and in the preface to *The Inquisitor* he insists that the scenes at its end are 'true history'.

We cannot say that Walpole is offering us counterfeit coin. The objection is not that what he describes is not true, but that it does not add anything to what we already know, or think we know. The thousands who came upon Benson's account of college life were thrilled by being able to recognise their ideal picture, entirely remote from their own lives, of what it *must* be like. It was not, so far as they were concerned, true to life, but it was true to an ideal. In the same way Walpole's cathedral town was a cosy confirmation of what people thought such a town ought to be.

The only way, however, to grasp what is really wrong with Walpole is to go to an author who does enlarge the experience instead of merely confirming a non-experience. Thomas Hardy's description of Dorchester, in *The Mayor of Casterbridge*, does the trick here:

> To birds of the more soaring kind Casterbridge must have appeared on this fine evening as a mosaic-work of subdued reds, browns, greys, and crystals, held together by a rectangular frame of deep green. To the level eye of humanity it stood as an indistinct mass behind a dense stockade of limes and chestnuts, set in the midst of miles of rotund down and concave field . . .[7]

But I need not go on. There is much more, and as Hardy gradually takes us into the town, every detail stands out with greater and greater sharpness. It is really most unfair to Hugh Walpole to set the two descriptions beside each other.

Benson and Walpole are what might be called high tosh. As for low tosh (I mean low, not vulgar; I am not concerned with nasties), a different critical posture is obviously called for, because, again, the context is different. You have to be severe on Benson and Walpole, since you expect better of them. Low tosh is another matter. There is so much of it that it is hardly worth quoting; let me, however, if only just for the pleasure of it, give a taste of two titles, both from Robert Hale's 1984 autumn catalogue. The first is Pamela Bennett's *Pearl*, and the blurb says:

> When she is eighteen, Pearl Cartwright's path is crossed by the ruthless Earl of Rossmorton and his sons, Bruce and James. Bruce rapes her and James walks in on the scene. Despite the circumstances, Pearl and he know they have fallen in love.
>
> Bruce dies, and the earl, half-mad with grief, forces James, now Viscount Maxton, to get possession of the child Pearl is about to have, using blackmail to gain his ends. But although James is now engaged to another woman, he and Pearl have become lovers, knowing their happiness cannot last. Rather than become a burden on him, Pearl flees,

unaware that the cruel earl has suddenly released James from the arranged marriage; how can the Viscount recover the woman he loves?

I leave the reader to pick out the clichés. It all has the impact of a nice warm bath, and no doubt will have done very well. More interesting is the blurb for *The Distance and the Dark*, by Nan Maynard, author of *Springtime of Tears* and other works:

> The family of prosperous industrialist Adrian Kempson appeared to have everything. His wife, Audrey, was a lovely amiable woman and they shared pride and joy in their three children – first-born prim, predictable Deirdre, the handsome, fair-haired boy, Matthew, and the youngest, beautiful, tempestuous Tessa. But Adrian's marriage had grown stale and he sought excitement with his secretary, Karen Grayson. Tessa at fourteen fell hopelessly in love with the husband of Deirdre – the ruthless Mark Ashton. Immediately following their marriage Mark and Deirdre went to Hong Kong, but on their return five years later, the desires of Mark and Tessa fuse and explode. Matthew Kempson loses the girl he loves because of his inability to control his lusty appetite for sex.
>
> Following an accident to Audrey which changes her attitude to life and her family, the Kempsons pick up the pieces and carry on.

The blurb tells us that the author lives in Maidenhead, where such goings-on are, of course, quite common, but always in the next road but one.

Between the high tosh and the low tosh we should expect to find a middling sort of tosh, and it certainly exists, but it is far harder to pin down. It would be tempting to put into this range the historical romance, for example. Yet to class all historical romances as tosh would be very unfair to a great many respectable novelists.

The 'traditional' English novel – the sort of novel for which the late Betty Trask left an enormous sum of prize money, bigger at one time than that offered by Booker McConnell – was nearly always based on one of a number of conflicts, principally between the individual on the one hand, and society on the other. Hero cannot marry heroine because they come from different social classes, or because the heroine has already lost her virginity, or perhaps because she is torn between her loyalty to a parent and her love for the hero, or simply because the social conventions prevent the two from communicating with each other: and it is the exploration of that conflict, and its eventual resolution, that gives the reader his or her satisfaction. And still does. The anguish of Hardy's Tess still gets us in the midriff, even though the cause of it is now quaintly outdated. We do not stop quaking for the happiness of Jane Eyre, just because the unreasonable conventions of her day prevented Mr Rochester from putting his wife into a mental home and getting a divorce. On the contrary, we are totally engaged from beginning to end. Nor do we sigh with impatience at the ridiculous innocence of the twelve-year-old hero of *The Go-Between*, who hasn't yet learned about sex, nor laugh at the horror of the eventual discovery which puts him off balance for life. We are thrilled. But the 'mainstream' novelist today, whose business is, I suppose, to reflect and illuminate the human condition here and *now*, cannot use these devices.[8]

It is therefore not surprising if the novelist who wants to exploit the traditional conflicts decides to use a historical setting, which readers can find credible. And, to judge by the respective sales figures of their books and those of the mainstreamers, the traditional conflicts are what most people still want.

Whether their novels can be called tosh depends on how they are handled, that is all. The interest in Nan Maynard's *The*

Distance and the Dark comes not from the plot, a pretty commonplace affair if you ask me, but from the vocabulary in which it is presented, at any rate in the blurb. Here every adjective or adverb does a pleasing clunk-click with its appropriate noun or verb, here each character has its expected characteristics. The wife is lovely and amiable, her youngest daughter not only beautiful but also tempestuous; Deirdre's husband is ruthless, Tessa's love for him hopeless, Matthew's appetite for sex lusty. And here are our old friends, Pride and Joy (love her, hate him).

Nan Maynard's many readers would expect as much. So long as she sees to it that her characters go on being like that, her readers are content; it would be dreadfully upsetting if fair-haired Matthew lost his looks, or if Mark Ashton suddenly melted with ruth. I find myself thinking of a visit I made many years ago to the old Siemens electrical factory in Woolwich. Some of the work was very tedious, and the management got concerned for the sanity of employees whose only task, day after day, was to wind the cores of electric motors with miles and miles of thin copper wire. So they tried shifting the women (they were all women, as it happened) to various different jobs so that they could take a bit of interest in what they were doing. The women became very agitated by this benevolence. They wanted what they knew, and demanded to be put back to their old benches, which they duly were. You could not have found a more contented bunch of people.

A corny story, no doubt, but then corn is what I am talking about. It is not necessarily to be despised.

For the desire – the hunger, almost – for repetition is not confined to factory workers or readers of light literature. The knowledge that the same dance steps, accompanied by the same sequence of notes or beats on a drum, can put dancers into a trance used to be special to anthropologists, but is now familiar to anyone who watches television or picks up one of those lush illustrated books about African tribespeople which pour out from the publishers these days. A mantra has an uplifting effect.

This has surely much to do with the distress of so many people when the Alternative Service Book was introduced. It meant that a worshipper going to the Holy Communion service could not be sure that the words he was going to hear this time would be the same as the words he heard last time; and unless the words are the same, there can be a strong feeling that they may not be valid, any more than the incantation of a magician is valid unless the proper words are used.

The repetition of the phrase is part of its point. To descend from the sublime to the ridiculous, the proceedings of the executive committee of the National Union of Teachers, which I had the pleasure of attending over some four years in the early 1960s, consisted very largely of certain traditional elements, introduced by successive speakers in traditional union language. One element of many debates was the need, in those days, to prevent members from going over to the rival National Association of Schoolmasters. Another was the many years of loyal and unstinting service which the speaker had given to the Union – a point often offered by speakers who were on the defensive, suggesting that though their arguments might be shaky, at least their *bona fides* was sound. A third, obviously powerful, element was the Needs of the Individual Child. All these and many other ploys, separately and together, made a gratifying pattern, and it was the skill and timing with which he selected and introduced the appropriate elements that brought the successful executive member his victory in debate.

I once made myself unpopular by suggesting privately that the actual words, having been heard pretty often before, were not really necessary to the business, and that much time could be saved if it could be conducted by a form of semaphore, for which a system could be devised with very little ingenuity. Each member had only to choose from the pigeonholes under his desk whatever symbol he wanted to introduce into the debate, everyone would know what he meant, and the committee could proceed immediately to the next symbol. Needless to say, the idea was not taken seriously; nor should it have been. Unless the ritual is gone through properly, there is no point in going through it at all.

I hope no one will accuse me of blasphemy when I mention in the same paragraph the Blessed Sacrament and the abracadabra of witches, to say nothing of the executive of the National Union of Teachers. The sacrament depends, as the Prayer Book puts it, on the merits and death of Christ, and on the faith of those who partake of it, not on a magic formula; indeed, the 1662 Book contains a lengthy passage, which is very seldom read, making it clear that unless the communicant has a quiet conscience, he should abstain. But obviously the ritual nature of the words is of enormous assistance to worship, and their familiarity a consolation to any who might doubt, in the words of the old (but not the new) Prayer Book, that 'Thou art the same Lord, whose property is always to have mercy.'

To descend, yet again, to the sublunary level: many comedians have relied much on repetition of the same catch-phrases to extract easy applause from their audiences. Tommy Handley did it brilliantly during the Second World War in his radio show 'It's That Man Again'. He and his scriptwriters devised a large collection of stock remarks which were repeated somewhere in every programme in which he appeared, and 'Can I do you now, sir?', the invariable entry line of Mrs Mopp the charlady, passed into common speech during and after the war. If she had failed to make the remark, listeners would have been disappointed and even angry. It was a self-generating cliché. Far from becoming bored by the sameness of Handley's series, listeners were delighted and would have felt badly let down if they had *not* been the same. He was heard by millions of people of all classes and became a national hero, demonstrating once again that we all love to hear the thing that we have heard before, and may in fact love it more the more often we manage to hear it.

Beachcomber (H. B. Morton), of the old *Daily Express*, did the same. If he had written 'Dr Strabismus of Utrecht' no doubt someone among his readers would have been quick to correct him. The proper form, as everyone knew, was: 'Dr Strabismus (whom God preserve) of Utrecht'. To leave out the parenthesis would have been in the nature of sacrilege.

Beachcomber's space was cruelly cut back, towards the end of his career, by some idiot of an editor. In our own day, his ashes are honoured by his spiritual heir, a greater man than he, Peter Simple (Michael Wharton) of the *Daily Telegraph*. Wharton always repeats the formula (sometimes quite a complicated one) each time he reintroduces one of his characters. It would be regarded as an affront to his readers if he did not mention, for example, that Alderman Foodbotham, chairman of the Tramways and Fine Arts Committee of Bradford City Council in the great days, was crag-visaged, grim-booted and iron-watch-chained; they know it very well, but they want to be told it again, just as they know, and must be told each time, that the Revd John Goodwheel is known as the Apostle of the Motorways and that Dr Ngrafta, of the former province of Gomboland, is the only practising witch-doctor who also holds a degree from the London School of Economics. (Wharton, incidentally, has a finer ear for cliché, and a greater understanding of its uses, even than Perelman had.)

So the delight in repetitions, in the fulfilment of expectances, can be found in many different forms, some noble, some frivolous, some satirical, some positively therapeutic. The desire to hear the same story over and over again, which we find in children, is also common in adults. Strangely, though, with grown-ups it does not always work. I have already pointed out that the use of the spoken catch-phrase is not only quite acceptable even to those whose finely-detailed nostrils curl whenever they think they have spotted a cliché in writing, but is

also actually a necessary lubricant for the wheels of social intercourse. Not so, I fear, in the case of the stories we tell each other over the evening pint. For example, I myself am not very good at telling stories of any sort, and have hardly more than half-a-dozen at my disposal. They include:
The Time I Backed the Winner of the Grand National
My Clash with Mrs Thatcher
How I Got to Meet T. S. Eliot
My Clash with Tony Crosland
and one or two others. Whenever I decide to take the old ego for a little run like this I have first to look very carefully round the table or down the bar in case I see someone to whom I may have told the story before, since everyone knows that to repeat a story of this sort to someone who has heard it before is a serious social sin. You can tell when you have committed it by the look on the face of even the politest sufferer. To commit it is nearly as bad as that other terrible sin, to tell a story to someone who has already told it to you. That is why it is always rash to tell set-piece jokes.

But again there are exceptions to this general rule. It is absolutely allowable to tell a story or anecdote which you and your friends know already, so long as it relates to a shared experience or to a common bit of folk-lore – for example:
The Time George Got Thrown Out of Claridges
What Old Tompkins said to the Features Editor
The Time Jim Got Thrown Out of the Pub
What Evans Really Said to Murdoch
and so forth. It was much the same in ancient Greece. People kept telling each other what Pallas Athene Really Said to Odysseus; the whole thing got more and more elaborate, until it was taken over by professionals, who declaimed it at length in public.

6 · Unfair to Hacks! *or* Tales of the Expected

The mention of Homer reminds me that it is time (high time, I seem to hear it murmured) to introduce Myles na gCopaleen, a pseudonym of Flann O'Brien, which is a pseudonym of Brian O'Nolan.

One of the brightest things in his 'Cruiskeen Lawn' column, which appeared between 1939 and 1966 in the *Irish Times*, was 'The Myles na gCopaleen Catechism of Cliché', described by him as 'a unique compendium of all that is nauseating in contemporary writing. Compiled without regard to expense or the feelings of the public. A harrowing survey of sub-literature and all that is pseudish, mal-dicted and calloused in the underworld of print.' The catechism opens thus:

Is a man ever hurt in a motor smash?
No. He sustains an injury.

> Does a man ever die from his injuries?
> No. He succumbs to them.
> Correct. But supposing an ambulance is sent for. He is put into the ambulance and *rushed* to hospital. Is he dead when he gets there, assuming that he is not alive?
> No, he is not dead. Life is found to be extinct *etc.*

Later we have this:

> What, as to the quality of solidity, imperviousness, and firmness, are facts?
> Hard.
> And as to temperature?
> Cold.
> With what do facts share this quality of frigidity?
> Print.

And later still:

> If a thing is fraught, with what is it fraught?
> The gravest consequences.
> What does one sometimes have it on?
> The most unimpeachable authority.[1]

And so on. In other parts of his Catechism na gCopaleen knocks the stuffing out of the pub cliché. (What, as he might himself ask, does he knock out of it? The stuffing. Try again. The living daylights? That's better.) But in the extracts above he gives his attention to two forms of cliché, both of them from the newspapers. The first is the circumlocutionary cliché; in the second and third quotations, he is knocking the portmanteau, or what Eric Partridge calls the 'doublet' – 'cold print', 'gravest consequences', 'unimpeachable authority'.

Both are devices of great age, going right back to ancient

Unfair to hacks!

times. The *Iliad* and the *Odyssey* are bursting with them. The circumlocutionary, or periphrastic, variety is the oldest in the business, in fact. Myles na gCopaleen's catechism is about the low sort. Homer's is the high sort. They should not be too difficult to distinguish. Here are some more, which I pick at random:

1. Death — grim reaper
2. Sea — restless wave
3. Sun — daystar; Phoebus' car
4. Cart — horse-drawn conveyance
5. Bus — itinerant vehicle

Easy! Actually 4 is from a newspaper, 5 from the later Wordsworth; 3 are both from Milton, though 'daystar' had already been used in the 1611 version of the New Testament;[2] 2 is from a hymn. I am not sure about 1 (Longfellow?) but it has now reached the colloquial-camp stage, and can be found in the better kinds of facetious journalism.

We label the low sort cliché, the high sort poetic diction.

In what, for lack of a better expression, I must call the dawn of language, one learns that periphrases were being used all the time, not so much because Adam and Eve had failed to carry out the Lord's instruction about the naming of every bird and beast — not because they couldn't think of enough words — but only because they couldn't grasp abstract ideas; they simply didn't know what they *were*. Thus if they wanted to talk about human life, a mysterious quality, they had to call it breath, and used the same word for the soul. For this reason it has been said, admittedly rather whimsically, that when Man first started talking, he talked poetry. (Even the Romans had the same word — *anima* — both for life and for the soul.)

Anyway, it is clear that the habit of calling a thing something different from what it actually is has a respectable enough past. By Homer's day they had got the whole technique to a fine art. Anyone could compile a Catechism of Homeric Cliché, na gCopaleen style.

Did the Trojan die?
No. He tasted the bitter earth.
And for whom was he himself the food?
For the dogs and the crows.
With the colour of what alcoholic beverage would you associate the sea?
With wine.
Correct. But how so?
It's the wine-dark sea, ennit?
Of course. And how is it sounding?
Many.
What effect did the wrath of Achilles have on a multitude of strong heroes? Surely it must have killed them?
No no.
What then?
It hurled their souls into Hades.
Would you say the Achaeans had a following wind?
I would not. The far-working Apollo sent them a favouring gale.
Excellent. Just one last question. In what respect do you associate the wake of their ship with a powerful opera star?
The dark wave sang loud about the stern.[3]

We laugh at na gCopaleen's examples, but we go on applauding Homer. This might seem rather hard on the poor fellows who produced those modern locutions. If Homer wrapped up the message with traditional verbiage, why shouldn't the journalists? Why should we groan at them? Presumably Homer's hearers did not groan as he once more described Achilles as 'the fleet of foot', or his work would surely not have come down to us. Give the hacks a chance.

A bit of a puzzle, eh? 'But surely,' you will argue, 'the Ancient Bard' (by which you mean Homer, but you didn't say

Homer, you said the Ancient Bard. Get on with it.) '—the bard was spouting *poetry*, dammit. All the difference in the world. Poetry is special. The modern journalist does not intone his news items to the twanging of a stringed instrument, as Homer did. There is no comparison, and it's absurd to try to make one.'

With respect, I still think there is a comparison to be made. The most important point is that in both cases a story is being told, and in both cases it is essential that the attention of the listener or reader is held, and that the story is believed. Homer sang of gods and heroes and it was therefore proper that his epic should be clothed in highly conventional, ritualised language, suitable to the status of his characters. Repetition was inevitable because it has to be borne in mind that in the first place the *Iliad* and the *Odyssey* were declaimed, and that the bard did not have a script. He needed to keep in his head many thousands of lines. So it is in the nature of oral epic that whoever compiled it should have a vast stock of conventional ways of describing particular actions, whether it might be a journey by sea, or a hand-to-hand fight between warriors, or the striking of a camp, or a hero's lament for a dead friend, or the phenomenon of death itself. But the possession of such a literary stock-cupboard was more than a mere convenience. Did it not, in the end, carry a sort of guarantee that the goods on offer were reliable? (Our product never varies.) Yes yes, the listeners must have said to each other, that's how it was, that's how it must have been, it has been told like that before, and it is a noble thing.

I put it in this way, not to diminish (who could?) the inexplicable splendour of the *Iliad*, but to get some sympathy for the task of the modern journalist. He, too, wants his story to be believed. How can he ensure the credulity of his readers? He puts it in a special language, a special formula, by which the readers are able to distinguish it from the sort of unconfirmed tittle-tattle they hear every day from their neighbours.

Homer's listeners would not think much of a bald announcement of the death of an Achaean – 'Achilles's ADC Patroclus was among the casualties' simply would not do. Nor would they want to hear that 'Diomed, well known for his racing stud, was the next speaker.' In the same way that they did not want the *Iliad* to sound like a news report, so the readers of the *Irish Times*, or whatever, are not going to be fobbed off with a news item phrased as though it were mere gossip. 'I hear he was badly hurt,' says the neighbour. Perhaps he was, perhaps he wasn't. 'The victim is understood to have sustained serious injuries,' says the paper. Ah, now you're talking. A far more reliable account, by the sound of it.

Newspaper editors have spent a lot of time in recent years trying to stop reporters writing like that. Their style-books have lengthening lists of 'Barred expressions' or 'Vogue words, to be avoided'. They have become victims of the Cult of Originality. They think, almost certainly wrongly, that a restricted code carries more conviction than an elaborated code. Their efforts are not always successful. Recalling the Israeli occupation of Southern Lebanon in 1982, the *Times* man does not write: 'It is two years now since the Israeli occupation of Southern Lebanon.' He writes: 'Nearly two years ago Israeli armour rumbled into Southern Lebanon on a sunny Sunday in June, 1982.'[4] 'Rumble' is the correct word for what tanks and armoured vehicles do, and the reader is entitled to it. Let 'em rumble.

When the President of the United States, in search of Irish ancestors, landed up in the small village of Ballyporeen, considerably disturbing its routine, the *Sunday Express* rose to the occasion like this:

> Never before [wrote its reporter] has the one and only thoroughfare of this sleepy Irish village seen such a frenzy of activity.

The single main street was not just that: it was the one and only thoroughfare; it was not just busy, it was in a frenzy of activity; and what else could such a small place be, except sleepy? All those phrases were from stock, but they were well enough suited to the occasion.

Pontrhydyfen was a different matter, calling for different treatment.

> In Pontrhydyfen, a tight-knit community north of Port Talbot where the two great passions are rugby and the career of Richard Burton, curtains were drawn in the windows of terraced houses.
> (*Daily Telegraph*, 6 August 1984)

To have called the Welsh village sleepy, the Irish tight-knit, would have been wrong in either case. The Welsh case was solemn, the Irish one absurd. Each reporter chose the right word.

Editors do no good when they try to persuade their staff away from word-combinations of this kind. The result may turn out to be a retreat from clarity, rather than a closer approach to it. The 'vogue words' they proscribe – 'juggernaut', 'snarl-up', 'confrontation' – very often have a distinct flavour which matches the way people see those things. But if the conscientious scribbler has to think of another word instead, he or she may lose the impact sought for.

Among words which have appeared in the proscribed lists of this sort are 'magnate', 'overwhelming' (of a majority), 'gutted' (of a fire, not a fish) and 'shambles'. There is nothing wrong with these words (with the possible exception of 'shambles', which is not specific enough, and could be used of anything from a nasty train accident to a rowdy council meeting). Everyone knows what a gutted building looks like; the alternative is 'burned out', which is neither better nor worse. But what is the alternative to an 'overwhelming majority'? Big, very big, very big indeed? The only sin which these words have committed, if sin it be, is that of having been often used; yet there are plenty of often-used words which have never attracted the stigma which these have. It is worth asking why. More reasonably, some words have been put on the lists of those 'to be avoided' – 'traumatic' and 'euphoria' are two which spring to mind – clearly because editors have felt that they are in danger of becoming devalued. Euphoria is something far more specific – or should be – than the vague and unrealistic optimism which it is often used to describe, and 'traumatic' has been known to be applied to situations in which, on closer examination, not many have been hurt after all; it should really be brought out only in the case of major earthquakes, rather than small ones. To ask for sparing use of such words suggests a praiseworthy desire to arrest their decline.

Obviously I am not making the absurd suggestion that newspapers should fill their columns with cliché after cliché. There are scores of them which diminish rather than intensify the message their writers are trying to convey, and scores of others which, deliberately or otherwise, conceal the fact that there is no message to give. I shall be giving some examples of both later on in this book. Here I am thinking of expressions which are discouraged by editors, and by some readers, simply because they are old, and therefore 'overdone'. But they are overdone only if they have stopped conveying the message. Age is not necessarily the criterion by which to judge the strength of a word or phrase.

The ancients knew this. Horace certainly did. Writing of 'novel terms', he advised young writers that 'Licence will be granted, if they are used with modesty'; in general, story-tellers should follow Homer. To young playwrights he said: 'Better to take a song of Troy than be the first to offer an unknown and unsung theme.' Horace also insisted that 'Words, *though* [my italics] new and of recent make, will win acceptance if they spring from a Greek fount and are drawn therefrom but sparingly.' Best to use familiar material, though you may modify it. And he likened the process to a tree renewing its leaves.[5]

To the ancients – and, for that matter, to anyone who wrote or read modern English in its first five centuries or so – such a proposition would seem almost self-evident. Why should it be thought that something new should stir the heart more readily than something old? Was not the reverse more likely to be the case? When Keats wanted to communicate the sense of desolation which he felt on hearing the nightingale – that awful feeling, which we all sometimes have, of being cut off from the sources of beauty – he did not rack his brains for some smart new image. He called in aid the Book of Ruth, whose tears on having to leave her native country had smitten generation after generation of Bible-readers. He knew that that would go home, and it did. When Charles Lamb wrote about a lost love, he likewise deliberately chose a Biblical echo – 'fairest among women,' he wrote, and his readers could be relied upon to grasp immediately, almost without thinking, the amalgam of beauty and saintliness thus conjured.[6] His publisher did not say to him: 'Mind if we sub that out, old boy? I mean, bit of a cliché, isn't it?' (I am told of a notable – and highly successful – 'back-bench man' in the sub-editors' room of the old *News Chronicle* in the late 1950s, who used to advise those under him: 'If it's a phrase you've heard before, you can bet your boots it's a cliché!')

Keats and Lamb were doing no more than following the ancient Greeks' approach to all the arts. Their development of the *kouros*, the sculpture of a naked youth, standing with arms at his side, one foot slightly in front of the other, is a good example, in which the conventional posture of the figure hardly varied from one work to the next. 'The Greeks', writes B. F. Cook in his excellent handbook on the subject, 'did not share the modern obsession for "originality".' The basic design of a Doric temple, as he points out, was fixed in about 700 BC and underwent two and a half centuries of gradual refinement before achieving its perfect form in the Parthenon.[7]

One could trace much the same sort of tradition in the iconography of painting. Here I would only encourage my reader to ask himself or herself why (for example) so many Venetian painters represented the female nude in the same old posture each time, reclining on couch, head on left side of picture, torso resting on right buttock, right elbow supporting head. Champions of the concept of originality presumably would not see the point, the point being, I should have thought, not so much that each successive artist thought that he could paint a woman in that particular posture better than the chap before (though no doubt he tried to do that too), as that each successive representation of such a woman purposely and self-consciously *referred back* to earlier examples, thus gradually building up a familiar image of great evocative power. So here is another whole range of 'clichés', but we still experience (do we not?) a certain thrill when we come across another Old Master offering us his own treatment of the same idea.

Anyway, Homeric circumlocution, and the constantly repeated use of a huge store of conventional word-groupings, were still the basis for narrative poetry in English not hundreds but thousands of years after Homer's time. Pope's translations of the *Iliad* and the *Odyssey* were a sort of modern up-dating of the technique, in the high style, where the sea becomes the 'watery plain', the woods 'sounding groves'; a favourable wind is 'indulgent gales', and a quiet girl is elevated to the status of a 'pensive nymph'.[8] It is somehow sad and ironic that, just as more people know Dryden's mock-heroic *Mac Flecknoe* than ever look at his serious heroic poetry, so we now remember Pope best for *The Rape of the Lock*, which made comic use of the devices which he himself handled so brilliantly in his translations of Homer. Leslie Stephen says disapprovingly that Pope's Homer 'became the accepted standard of style for the best part of a century'.[9] (He might have added that Spenser and Milton, particularly Milton, had almost as much influence.) The emphasis in this long tradition of English poetic diction was on periphrasis, rather than on repetition, and it was not used just for the telling of heroic tales. Thus we have the mellifluous Oliver Goldsmith, in his description of nothing more heroic than a village dance, calling it a 'mirthful maze', and the old women 'dames of ancient days', and giving a pretty picture of an old man taking the floor:

> And the gay grandsire, skilled in gestic lore,
> Has frisked beneath the burthen of threescore.[10]

Inevitably this art of periphrasis sooner or later got itself into ridiculous places, far removed from the austere brilliance of Pope. Dr John Armstrong, of Edinburgh, began his treatise on health by apostrophising the Goddess Hygeia for all the world like Milton appealing to his Heavenly Muse at the start of *Paradise Lost*, and put his advice to the overweight (less food, more exercise, early rising) thus:

> Choose leaner viands, ye whose jovial make
> Too fast the gummy nutriment imbibes;
> Choose sober meals; and rouse to active life
> Your cumbrous clay; nor on the enfeebling down
> Irresolute, protract the morning hours.[11]

Obviously a stop had to be put to this sort of thing, which is exactly what Coleridge and Wordsworth tried to do.

But if periphrasis is to be defined as describing a thing in a roundabout way (often in terms of something else), it is plain that poetry could not do without it. Wordsworth's claim that 'A large portion of the language of every good poem can in no respect differ from that of good prose', obviously untenable when he wrote it, could not be sustained even by himself, and his own verse gradually became more intricate and what was naturally thought of as 'poetic'. The American scholar Herbert Lindenberger, in an appendix to his book on *The Prelude*,[12] gives a pleasant example of the process, where Wordsworth changes a fairly simple image of the Children of the Spring – 'plants, insects, beasts in field, and birds in bower' (1805) into a far more elaborate image of the creatures

> Piping on boughs, or sporting on fresh fields
> Or boldly seeking pleasure nearer heaven
> On wings that navigate cerulean skies. (1850)

It was not uncommonly supposed by critics in the second half of the nineteenth century that Wordsworth had freed English poetry from 'artificial' locutions of just this sort, but of course he had done nothing of the kind. (One asks what 'natural' poetry is.) Matthew Arnold (who had his own views on translating Homer) does not say that the Scholar Gipsy has left *Oxford*: he calls Oxford 'the studious walls', which is artificial enough; and instead of reminding the reader that the Scholar Gipsy died a long time ago, he movingly elaborates the idea:

> And thou from earth art gone
> Long since, and in some quiet churchyard laid!
> Some country nook, where o'er thy unknown grave
> Tall grasses and white flowering nettles wave –
> Under a dark red-fruited yew-tree's shade.

Those marvellous lines were written in 1855, five years after *The Prelude* in its Miltonised version was published. Yet twelve years after that, F. J. Furnivall, writing probably from the studious walls of Trinity Hall, Cambridge, was praising the eighteenth-century antiquarian Bishop Percy for having 'led the van of the army that Wordsworth afterwards commanded, and which has won us back to nature and to truth'. Such nonsense.[13]

But let us return to the subject of modern journalism, which is where this chapter started. The first point which has to be made is that periphrasis, or circumlocution, or whatever one likes to call it, is a natural (I almost said indestructible) instinct in anyone who uses language, whether written or spoken. Unless we are to confine ourselves to the vocabulary of the instruction manual and the police report – and even these have their particular modes – there can be no such thing as plain English, nor is there any such thing as an 'objective' way of telling a story, as every journalist knows.

The second point is that, until the advent of the novel, the proper vehicle for narrative was always thought of as verse, rather than prose, whether its aim was to elevate the mind, or merely to entertain. (The historians come in a different category.) There were two main streams. The narrative designed to elevate or enlarge the soul used the form of the literary epic, which was its noblest manifestation; the oral tradition was carried on in the form of the ballad. Today both these traditions are dead. General literacy has killed the oral tradition, and as for the literary epic, poetry hardly ever speaks to us in this way any more, having other things to do. So the modern equivalent of the 'high' verse narrative is the serious novel; that of the 'low' verse narrative is the newspaper report. It is not without significance, incidentally, that newspapermen never talk about reports, but always about 'stories'.

I am thinking here of the mass-circulation newspaper report, rather than what is to be found in 'serious' papers, though not too much need always be made of the distinction. The newspaper-reading public, which means pretty well everyone who can read, wants stories, and I suggest that our desire for stories is different in no fundamental way from our not-too-distant ancestors' desire for a broadsheet or a ballad. In both cases certain requirements have to be met. It must be about something which is said actually to have happened; it must carry the ring of truth; and it must in one of a number of ways evoke a sense of wonder or of surprise.

It is amusing to find F. J. Furnivall, whom I have already quoted in another connection, talking rare sense of the value of ballads to 'the students of history, of society and manners, of thoughts and customs' of former days, describing them as:

> These light hand-glasses [which] reflect for us many a feature of the times that is lost in the crowded scenes which larger mirrors, hung at other angles, present to our view; and without the sight of the ballad pictures, as well as the larger and more formal ones of professed histories, State papers, memoirs, and treatises, we cannot know faithfully . . . the lineaments of the ages that have preceded us.[14]

Furnivall was surely describing here, with more precision than he could possibly have realised, the function of a modern popular newspaper story, in recording 'many a feature of the times' not to be found in State papers. Obviously the heroes of the ballads were often different from those of Grub Street. They were monarchs, knights, giants, witches, travellers, murderers, imprisoned maidens, young princes who had lost their way or who had fallen on evil days. We too have our monarchs and our murderers, but we also have heart surgeons, football managers, wicked tycoons, and the fabulous beings who inhabit the world of entertainment. To that list we must also add animals, children and babies. A glance through the front page leads of (say) the *Daily Express* over a randomly-chosen month reveals a half-magic world as bizarre in its own way as almost anything that can be read in the ballads of Robin Hood, Sir Patrick Spens, Sir Gawaine or the Carl of Carlisle. 'Killer haunts grave of girl victim', we find as the lead for 30 July 1984: 'Bizarre police vigil after tomb outrage'. A few days later, on successive days, the heroism of two different infants is celebrated, both under the surgeon's knife. On August 16 the banner headline proclaims a Homeric theme: 'Death of a hero', it says. But it turns out to be a dog: 'Courageous police dog Yerba was shot dead during a bank raid yesterday as he saved five lives. Gunmen callously pumped three bullets into the Alsatian . . .' The same morning the *Standard* takes up the theme: 'Othello, heir to Yerba's courage', it says, naming the successor to the wonder dog. On a grander level was the *Sunday Express*'s splash headline one morning the previous May: 'Agony of Pets in Picket Terror'.

The Delilah theme gets suitable treatment in the *Daily Star* on 10 July 1984: 'Sex for Secrets: Blonde Spy Set Trap for Airman . . . A sexy spy bewitched young airman Paul Davies into giving away NATO secrets, a court heard yesterday.' Three weeks later, when we read of the meeting between the beautiful Mata Hari and the airman's mother, we are back in the world of Guinevere and the lovely damosel, daughter of King Peleus, Elaine herself.

Nothing could be more natural than that those who tell the stories today should borrow, consciously or unconsciously, some of the techniques of the versifiers. They worked in the past, and there is no reason why they should not work now. For example, the balladmongers naturally sought to exaggerate the size of their characters, making their dwarfs diminutive, their giants huge. (The Carl of Carlisle had eyes a span apart, and drank fifteen gallons of wine at a draught.) A similar obsession with size can be detected in newspaper stories today:

> The miners' dispute burst into its worst-ever day of hate yesterday. Up to 10,000 pickets besieged a tiny pit village howling 'scab' at the workers and 'whore' at their wives. And last night the giant Ravenscraig steel plant in Scotland was set to become the new flashpoint.
>
> (*Daily Star*, front page, 3 May 1984)

(Note 'tiny', 'howl', 'giant'.)

> Nine-year-old Rajaad Julron (only 4 ft), the tiny victim of a vicious East-end attack.
> (*Standard*, 16 August 1984)

In the *News of the World* of August 19 we read of a randy gamekeeper, who stunned villagers by getting a court order allowing him to stay in the village: 'A leading member of the tiny community said bitterly yesterday: "He has no sense of shame."'

Again, the descriptions of people and actions in such stories have an almost unvarying vocabulary, reminiscent of oral epic. Rapists are vicious, dead babies tragic, parents mourn or grieve or, if a child is saved, weep unashamedly. ('As her eyelids fluttered open and her tiny hands started to move, [her] parents fell into each other's arms and wept unashamedly' – *Daily Express*, 2 August 1984.) Increases are dramatic, smiles are broad if worn by villains, beaming if found on children, and villains bring a reign of terror to tiny communities. Blondes are stunning or striking, and tennis superstar Bjorn Borg's new love is teenage beauty Jannicke Bjorling. We are in the linguistic demesne of wide-browed Homer, where swift Achilles strove with great Agamemnon over the fair-cheeked Briseis, and the white-armed Hera looked on. These ritual pairings of words have a long ancestry, and are not to be mocked; nor do I mock them.

Thus, though newspaper themes are nearer the ballad than the epic – and, inevitably, put in a lower key than either – even the devices of serious poetry are still to be found, in vestigial form, in such newspapers as those from which I have been quoting. Another of these devices is that of personification, natural to the Greeks, and much exploited by eighteenth-century English poets, sometimes to a slightly absurd extent. Collins in his *Ode to Evening* made evening into a shy maiden whose ear he hoped to soothe by his verses, and surrounded her with a crowd of (presumably female) entities:

> The pensive Pleasures sweet
> Prepare thy shadowy car,

and

> While Spring shall pour his showers, as oft he wont,
> And bathe thy breathing tresses, meekest Eve! . . .
> While sallow autumn fills thy lap with leaves . . .
>
> So long, regardful of thy quiet rule,
> Shall Fancy, Friendship, Science, smiling Peace,
> Thy gentlest influence own,
> And love thy favourite name!

– while George Crabbe managed in *The Library* to get Comedy and Folly to engage in personal combat.[15] Coleridge was severe on Gray for having called the sun Phoebus, which he declared to be 'hackneyed, and a schoolboy image', but excused Renaissance poets for having done the same thing, which, however, continued to be done while Coleridge pronounced, notably by Keats ('Where Palsy shakes a few, last, sad grey hairs' etc.). The most common personifications in newspapers are, traditionally, Fear and Terror,[16] which have been given much to do over the years, together with their sister Fury.

> Fury erupted last night in the village at the centre of the hunt for the Fox.
>
> (*Daily Star*, 30 July 1984)

But I rather liked this variant from the *Sussex Express* of 10 August 1984: 'Apathy hit Lewes Carnival on Saturday' – though the reporter rather spoilt the effect by adding 'both from the public and those taking part', as though apathy were a missile, rather than a draped female figure. (The main headline on the same page, incidentally, was 'Crackdown hits home work', which meant that local government cuts had stopped more council houses being built. But the language of headlines is a different subject in its own right.)

Sports writing is, or was, a rich field for heroic circumlocution. The ripest example I have seen dates from 1939, and is quoted in his *Dictionary of Clichés* by Eric Partridge, who in turn got it from Frank Whitaker's presidential address to the Institute of Journalists the year before. I cannot resist quoting it yet again:

> Stung by this reverse, the speedy left-winger propelled the sphere straight into the home custodian's hands. He found it a rare handful, and was glad to let it go.

This certainly carries with it some of the flavour of an encounter on the windy plains of Troy. One is reminded, too, of Gray's familiar lines from his *On a Distant Prospect of Eton College:*

> Who foremost now delights to cleave
> With pliant arm, thy glassy wave?
> The captive linnet which enthrall?
> What idle progeny succeed
> To chase the rolling circle's speed
> Or urge the flying ball?

This style of sports writing used to be known as the Erstwhile Cantab school, in memory of the unknown reporter who applied this term to one of the players, an old Cambridge man. He had used his name in the previous sentence, and had wanted, like any eighteenth-century versifier worth his salt, to find an elegant variant. Mr Whitaker was very hard on the man who called the ball a sphere and the goalkeeper a custodian, and asked of the passage he quoted: 'Can anything be said in its favour?' Whether it can or not, there is less of this style to be found on the sports pages nowadays, though occasionally one comes across a faint echo, as in this account in the *Daily Telegraph* of 6 August 1984:

> Britain gained its second gold medal of the Los Angeles Olympics yesterday when its coxed four rowing crew surged past their American rivals to win a final fought out on misty Lake Casitas.

That 'misty' is surely a Homeric epithet if ever there was one. Compare:

> Where cold Dodona lifts her holy trees
> Or where the pleasing Titaresius glides.
>
> (*Iliad*, ii. 750–1[17])

Lower down the same column we come across an interesting cliché which I thought was usually confined to the City pages: 'But they showed their ability by *clawing back* the lead in the last 500 metres' – if you want to call it a cliché.

I was glad to see the excellent Mr Whitaker, in the address mentioned above, defending certain phrases which he found barred in the style-books, including one which na gCopaleen had laughed at.

> Other forbidden phrases [said Mr Whitaker] – to take a few at random – are 'date back to', 'grow smaller', 'more or less certain', 'totally destroyed' and 'sustain injuries' . . . I maintain that there is nothing wrong with any of these phrases . . . they are idioms embedded in the language, and a hundred style sheets won't uproot them . . . We must keep a sharp eye on these diehards of the style sheet who are continually trying to drive useful phrases out of circulation and make language self-conscious.[18]

Just what I was saying myself. But Mr Whitaker loses me when he speaks of

> Rubber-stamp words that appear with such maddening frequency not only in our headlines and on contents bills, for which there is some excuse, but also in our reporters' copy, for which there is none.

With the greatest respect to the admirable Mr Whitaker (who was editor of *John O'London's Weekly* at the time), I suggest not only that there is every excuse, but also that newspaper readers actually like 'rubber-stamp words'. Mr Whitaker quoted a journalist in a novel by Gilbert Frankau who is made to say:

> When I've got anything important to tell the public I always tell it to them in clichés, because that's the way they understand it best

– a remark which, said Mr W, made him 'prickle with shame and indignation'. I don't think he needed to feel shame. But then, to beg the question again, it depends what you think a cliché is.

When we were children we loved to be told stories, and the ones we liked best were the ones we had been told already. What parent has not been driven slightly dotty by children wanting to hear exactly the same story they heard the night before, and in exactly the same words? To vary them invites correction, whether the story comes from a book, or out of the parent's head. The circulation figures for the popular newspapers suggest that these childish pleasures persist into adulthood. The successful reporter surely knows this. It is inevitable, therefore, that he should be dealing much of the time in stereotypes. He is also dealing in truth. His stories, unlike those told to children, must be about something which

Unfair to hacks!

actually took place. Here the most successful journalist of all, whether reporter or sub-editor, is the one who can recognise the stereotype when he or she sees the bare story. If he can make his characters fit the attributes expected of them so much the better. This easily explains the large number of 'stunning' blondes, 'vicious' or 'callous' criminals and 'tragic' widows 'mourning' their 'heroic' husbands, who people the columns of the popular Press; and if the tragic widow can by some smaller or greater stretch also be described as stunning, then stunning let her be. Nor are the themes chosen so very different from those which we find in the ballads or the folk-tales, given our own cooler, more 'scientific' attitude towards signs and wonders. As I have said, it is all on a more prosaic level: lions no longer whelp in the streets, or if they do, the report will not seek a supernatural reason. (It takes at least a bolt of lightning for that.)[19] Meanwhile villains thrive and have to be exposed, blood flows, children are abandoned, maidens are jilted, innocence suffers and hopes to be rewarded, the mighty take counsel and the rich feast in their high halls, just as their ancestors did. It would be surprising if some journalists, in their effort to make the facts of the story fit the stereotypes, did not give way to a temptation to stretch them too far. Did the bereaved widow truly weep? Did she really say the words attributed to her? Perhaps not. But did the doomed Sir Patrick Spens really say to his seamen:

Make ready, make ready, my merry men all

as they prepared to set sail for Noroway over the foam? And did Hero really mourn Leander by 'tearing her golden hair', and saying to the Hellespont:

Accursed river! That art still
A foe to every maid
Since Helen fair in thee was drowned[20]

in any language? Well, probably. Or something like it. Unfortunately Hero was not available for interview at the time of going to press.[21] (News editor to reporter: 'Well, what would she have said?')

One can usually guess when the modern equivalent of the golden-haired Hero is being quoted in her absence, so to speak. Example:

> Blonde Caroline Fairfax said later: 'I will now be able to realise the dearest of my desires. I can at last become the mother of my darling Eric's child. I thank justice and my lawyers.'

That is from an actual cutting, except that I have changed the names, because the popular newspapers are remarkably sensitive about charges of this nature, and it is just possible that the lady really did say something like that. Perhaps it was just a free translation (the lady was not English). There are degrees of freedom in these matters, anyway. People are not often so obliging (unless they are public figures) as to give good quotes. An aggrieved person might say he was 'very upset' about what had happened to him, but this is poor stuff for the storyteller. Telephone conversation: *Reporter*, 'Would you say that this was a shocking outrage?' – 'Yes I would.' 'Were you frightened?' – 'I certainly was.' 'Terrified?' – 'Well, I suppose I was.' 'Are you going to sue?' – 'Do you think I should?' etc., etc. *Quote in paper*: 'Mr Jones said at his home yesterday: "I was terrified. It was a shocking outrage, and I am thinking of suing."'

I may well be asked why I bother to defend such tosh. My aim is neither to defend it nor to attack it, but to identify some of its sources and to explain, partly at any rate, how it comes to exist. What I will defend, and gladly, is its language and its style, which seem to me to be entirely appropriate for what it is trying to do. In another place, those particular word-combinations would rightly be condemned. As Randolph

Quirk would say, it's all a question of context. In this context, to dismiss them as clichés is entirely to misread their function, and is beside the point.

Perhaps it is worth adding that the habit of chasing after the handiest stereotype is not always confined to the gutter press. 'A Stunned Village Flies its Flag at Half Mast', I read on the morning after the explosion at the Abbeystead waterworks, Lancashire, on 23 May 1984. (Picture caption: 'The roofless chamber of death'.) The story began:

> The flag on the church tower in St Michael's on Wyre flew at half mast yesterday over a little community shocked by tragedy.

This was in *The Times*, whose reporter later pointed out that

> Mr Frank Hogarth, of St Michael's, was all set to go on the tour [of the waterworks which exploded] with his wife Linda and two children, Stephen, aged 10, and Catherine, aged eight. He then discovered that Stephen had not done his homework and as a punishment the children stayed at home . . . Other villagers thought the casualty list would have been longer if the village bowling club had not been playing that night.

Every reporter knows that after an accident there are two types of person to be sought. One is the person whose luck saved him from going on the trip at the last minute. The other is the unlucky one who took advantage of a late cancellation . . . The *Times* man scored half-marks here.

7 · . . . and some nasty ones

Time, then, for yet another definition. Children go on wanting the same stories till they are tired of them. A cliché is a phrase or idea which some of us have got tired of quicker than others. For us it is a cliché, for the others it is not. (All clichés, by the way, are mere.)

At least this is better than some I have heard. The dislike of anything which has either been used a great deal already, or happens to be much in use at the moment, has led some writers into a strange mishandling of the word.

> Let us consider the word 'tabloid', the cliché that found a niche in the English language,

writes Philip Howard in *The Times*. This is indeed enough to give clichés a bad name, or at least the wrong one. Admittedly people tend to be suspicious of '-oid' words, which is only natural, since they are often used by writers who want to give their message a quasi-scientific authority; but there is not much wrong with the innocent 'tabloid', which, as the learned Mr Howard points out, started life as the trade name for a kind of pill, and, as he says, 'is an encouraging example of the way that language works'.

There is also a frequent confusion between the cliché on the one hand and, on the other, the 'received idea', to use Flaubert's expression, so that the word becomes a handy projectile for launching at any notion which is being commonly bandied about.

> It is a cliché (and also, I feel, a major untruth) that genius is never recognised in the lifetime of its possessor.
> (Auberon Waugh, *Spectator*, 2 June 1984)

Mr Waugh is not implying that a cliché is necessarily untrue, only that it is a remark which is often made, just as 'tabloid' is a word which is often used. But this example is not really a cliché at all; it is a mere platitude.

Out of something over 880 entries in Jacques Barzun's excellent translation of Flaubert's *Dictionnaire des Idées Reçues*,[1] fewer than a quarter (just over 200, on my count) can be called clichés in the generally agreed sense of 'worn-out' images or pairings of words or of ideas. The rest, amounting to 600 or so entries, are platitudes, pruderies and popular *bêtises*. All architects are idiots, forget to put in the stairs. All bachelors' apartments are in a perpetual mess, with a smell of tobacco, and women's garments strewn about: 'a search would reveal amazing things'. Flaring nostrils are a sign of lasciviousness. Anger stirs the blood and it is therefore healthy to yield to it now and again. Undecipherable handwriting is an indication of deep science, e.g., in doctors' prescriptions.

Planning it, Flaubert wrote to a friend:

> Such a book, with a good preface in which the motive would be stated to be the desire to bring the nation back to tradition, order and sound convention – all this phrased so that the reader would not know whether or not his leg was being pulled – such a book would certainly be unusual, even likely to succeed, because it would be entirely up to the minute.[2]

The surprising thing about Flaubert's dictionary is that so much of it still seems up-to-the-minute even now, more than 130 years later. (People are still saying the same thing about architects. Doctors, of course, have been rumbled.) A sort of attempt to up-date it was made a few years ago when Henry Root (alias William Donaldson) wrote *Henry Root's World of Knowledge*,[3] a straight crib of Flaubert's idea; but I believe it did not do particularly well, possibly because too many people did in fact 'not know whether their legs were being pulled'; I have certainly heard it being taken seriously by one or two intelligent people. Actually this probably served Henry Root right for meanly not having acknowledged his debt to Flaubert (except by naming him among a list of sixty so-called 'contributors'), and for lifting (also without acknowledgement) bits out of newspapers which sound funny only if the reader is drunk at the time, a bad test for humour. (It also gave him a taste of his own medicine. A few years earlier he had produced *The Henry Root Letters*[4] – spoof letters to various public figures, the joke being that they *didn't* see the joke, and answered back. There is no answer to a spoof encyclopaedia.)

Many of Flaubert's clichés (the use of the word in this sense had not arrived in his day, of course) are simple pairings: headlong progress, religion of our fathers, overwhelming evidence. Champagne is sampled, congratulations are hearty, and the most beautiful parts of a woman's body are made of alabaster. Ambition is mad or noble. Stallions are always fiery. The literary sobriquets and circumlocutions make a minor category: you must say 'missive' (nobler than letter), 'precincts' for neighbourhood, 'varsity' for university, 'alpha and omega' for beginning and end, 'newshound' for journalist. All women from the Orient are 'odalisques', and swallows are harbingers of spring from a far-off strand.

But most of them are verbal rather than written – the sort of thing which might be heard round a bourgeois dinner-table. Jacques Barzun, in a perceptive introduction to his version of the dictionary, points out that it

> frequently derides ... the specially French as against the European or world outlook; the stay-at-home timidity and love of the familiar which, although a universal trait, is reinforced in France by a tradition of complacency that dates back to Louis XIV.[5]

He also declares that the French language,

> despite its marvellous power of combining force and subtlety, is traditionally a language of clichés. Ready-made expressions abound and are to be preferred, indeed it is not licit to break them up, it is *'extravagant'*.

Flaubert, says Barzun, was mocking 'words and acts which deviate from the norm without undermining the "bases"'; and he thinks that one of the causes of the timidity shown up by Flaubert is to be found in the French education system:

> French text-books repeat the same views, offer the same extracts, and, lest the student should rashly venture on a perception of his own, guide him with footnotes to the correct criticism of the text.[6]

That was written in 1954, since when the French schools have undergone great changes, as have our own; indeed, it was partly the reaction to just such a way of teaching, as I have already suggested, that led to our present idiotic view that 'original' ideas are somehow supposed to be more valuable than 'second-hand' ones. ('*Neologisms*: The ruin of the French language,' says the cynical Flaubert.)

We have all been to dinner parties at which the conversation, if recorded on tape, would be found to consist almost entirely of clichés of various sorts, particularly if the diners were not very well known to one another. An exchange of agreed ideas, in a shared argot, is among the most effective ways of developing an acquaintance or confirming a friendship. 'I like So-and-so,' we say; 'He's got the same ideas as I have.' By their clichés ye shall know them.

Flaubert's diners tend to be 'clever'. When they light a candle, they say '*Fiat lux*' to show that they are well-educated people, call Shakespeare the Bard, and refer to laughter as Homeric;[7] when someone arrives who has been expected, they say '*Ecce homo*.'[8] Such things are as harmless as birdsong. They are identification signals, which will fail in their purpose if they are not recognised; the last thing, therefore, which they need to be is original. They are, as I have said earlier, no more than social lubricants, and are extremely useful. If, tiring of them, or finding them not to our taste, we were to leave Flaubert's table and go (sorry, *repair*) to an inn, we might well find ourselves giving and receiving an entirely different set of signals, better suited to the company.

> What's your poison, dear boy? Speak now, I'm in the chair.
>
> Well, I mustn't linger, or I shall be in the doghouse. The old woman will be making with the rolling pin.
>
> Treat 'em rough, I say. Come on, drag up a pew.
>
> Well, if you twist my arm.

> Short and strong, or weak and watery?
>
> I have to go easy, my quack has given me the red light.
>
> Liver?
>
> No, ticker. (etc., etc.)[9]

This, of course, is the pub cliché at its most inane, and I reproduce it (one could go on ad lib, or to the crack of doom, or till closing time) only to make the point that its function is different in no particular from that of the clichés exchanged at the candlelit table we have just left. They are both types of the spoken cliché, and spoken clichés all have one aim in common, whatever their intellectual level – that is, to unite the speakers.

The written cliché is an entirely different matter; its function might well be not to unite, but to divide; to conceal, rather than to communicate; or to delude, rather than to enlighten. Consider this fragment:

> In many respects, 1951 has been a turning point in the development of the Major Project on Mutual Appreciation of Eastern and Western Cultural Values, although no radical changes have been introduced. Now that the Project has been under way for four years, the relative importance of activities designed to launch it and to enlist the support needed for its implementation has diminished, while on the other hand, studies in depth and projects likely to yield more lasting results have received greater emphasis, a growing volume of material has been disseminated through more carefully prepared channels, and institutions whose regular activities contribute to the aims of the Major Project have been set up, or strengthened where they already existed.[10]

It is not worth counting up the clichés in this paragraph. They lean out of the page and shake the reader by the hand. But there is no doubt about their purpose, which is to delude and to conceal. What they conceal, or try to conceal, is the fact that a vaguely-conceived project, agreed by delegates at one of those painful international conferences (in this case, of Unesco), has been on the secretariat's desks for four years and nothing particular has happened, though much work has been done. Enthusiasm has been sought and not necessarily found, horns have been drawn in, committees have been strengthened, and the amount of paperwork shifted (or growing volume of material) has been terrific, but the Cultural Values have remained much where they were. The aim is to keep the next meeting of delegates happy, particularly those of the nation which put up the original resolution.

Richard Hoggart, who was director general of Unesco for some years, has written feelingly about this 'extraordinarily elaborate, abstracted style, yet one full of dead metaphors' which 'soon becomes an organisational litany', and likens it to governmental gobbledegook on the one hand ('a sort of verbal morning dress') and, on the other, to the clichés of undertakers designed to avoid saying someone is dead.[11]

That concealment is the aim there can surely be no question. The sorely-tried international civil servants have been saddled with an impossible task, yet to admit that it is impossible would not only be impolite; it would endanger the whole outfit. So they have to fudge it.

Hoggart says that the conventional phrasing, of which he gives some instances himself,[12] castrates thought. It is possible that some people working for such international agencies are eventually lulled by this insidious music; I can only say, from the few meetings I have had with them, that the best of them are entirely aware of what they are doing, and why they have to do it.

One does not have to go to Paris, or even to Whitehall, to find euphemistic prose like that of Unesco reports, though seldom on so grand a scale.

> With reference to your holding of United Paperclips £2 Capital Gains Distribution shares, I have received a request from our Stock Offices Services branch concerning a credit voucher on that holding of £105.50 which was recently placed in your account. They require a sight of the voucher which we are unable to trace at this branch. I would therefore be grateful if you could let me know whether you are holding this voucher . . .

(In other words, for God's sake help me, I've lost this certificate, and someone wants to see it, and *have you got it?*) Some bank managers put it more plainly:

> A search of the papers we hold has failed to locate this certificate.[13]

(I've looked *everywhere*.) At least in these instances there is no attempt to conceal the truth, only to make it sound less harsh, as though failing to locate something were not quite as bad as actually losing the wretched thing. It is also conceivable that if the bank had actually found something, they would also write that they had *located* it; for this is the business cliché. It gives dignity to the banker's calling, but it does more: it distances him from his customer, as surely as the grill at the counter. We can be fairly certain that a bank manager never wrote to his mother like that, though there may be one or two who do.

Parent, writing to her daughter's head teacher to explain that the child is ill and cannot go to school:

> I regret that due to a temporary indisposition June is prevented from attendance today.

That is a nice case of someone trying to use what she imagines to be someone *else's* clichés – an instance of the 'inclusive' cliché this time, unlike the bank manager's effort, which is plainly 'exclusive'. But consider this, from a recent book about bereavement.

> Adult to Adult Pair Bonds
> To adult pair bonds, each partner brings an inner image of such relationships and how they should be – a constellation of cognitive symbols with memories and affects attached.
> The relationship between the married couple takes many complex forms. It is built upon many levels. It is, as well, a special subsystem of the family group, and it is influenced by, and a reflection of, the broader social system. Yet it represents the interacting of individual dynamic forces on each partner.[14]

The fascinating thing about this excerpt is that the author is actually trying to help ordinary people, who have lost someone dear to them and want to know how to cope. But she is also writing for counsellors, that is to say, for fellow-professionals, so she has to wheel on the professional, exclusive clichés like cognitive symbols, the broader social system and the interacting of individual dynamic forces. (Never mind if the counsellors don't understand it either, she has made her position clear, so to speak.)

It is just possible that this author did not know what was happening here. Of course there is a much simpler way of saying what she says in that paragraph, in so far as she says anything at all worth saying. But *did she know this*? Or was it a simple case of that dreadful form of self-hypnosis which afflicts so many professional experts who can no longer say or think anything except in exclusive, circuitous language? It is hard to say. The reader must draw his own conclusions.

The following sentence was written by a conscientious civil servant at – or possibly by an academic seconded to – the old Ministry of Housing and Local Government:

> The national analysis of electoral returns suggests that there exists a relationship between electoral activity and the degree of rurality of the area.[15]

Here, surely, is a clear and simple case of self-hypnosis, very hard to cure. There is no attempt to conceal anything, no pulling of the wool, not even a need to show expertise, as there was in the previous quotation. It is part of a statistical appendix to a Government-commissioned report, and is not even signed. In fact its author was obviously trying to be as precise and helpful as he could. But the poor fellow could not say, which was what he meant, 'The remoter the area the fewer the candidates, in relation to the number of seats.' He had to say 'degree of rurality'. ('Electoral activity' can just be excused, as it is measured by a formula explained earlier in the appendix.) For him 'degree of rurality' was a perfectly normal way of writing.

We can guess that, for the author of the next example, this was not normal writing at all:

> We cannot regard this communication of novelty in the tissues of society as merely a continuation of the primitive social metabolism, Melinowski's 'phatic communion' of early man, except in its emotional satisfactions. In content and function it is a transforming rather than a stabilising process. And it may work with equal force whether the ideas communicated are sound or unsound. In fact, hitherto the bad currency has too often driven out the good.[16]

It is from his contribution to a rather classy year book bringing together the thoughts of a large number of scholars from all over the world – quite a challenge, and a temptation to show off. This is writing with a Canterbury cap on. But here is a much more interesting case:

The difficulty here is that deeply rooted ideas about equality of opportunity refer, by implication, to the present educational milieu which is still very hierarchical, authoritarian and mirrors the value judgments made on various occupational niches by present society. This is hardly likely to be the best means for investing our potential in the future.

The poverty implicit in an approach wherein a measurement of IQ determines the subsequent parcelling out of the appropriate experience drawn from a few alternatives does not do us proud.[17]

Styles of writing are like faces. Some are beautiful, some homely or plain, some strongly marked; some are so stiff with obscurantist jargon that they can hardly be recognised as faces at all; some wear strange masks covering who knows what behind them. The kindest thing one can say about the sample above is that it is deeply unattractive. Can we read the character behind it? Again, I am not worried about whether what the author is saying here is true. The point he is making is arguable and is, indeed, often argued. But what sort of man is it who can write about 'mirroring the value judgments made on various occupational niches' and 'the poverty implicit in an approach wherein' etc.?

There are several possibilities:
1. He is trying to impress his colleagues, and these are conscious clichés, with just a hint of deception about them. (He is not, after all, saying anything new.)
2. He thinks that this is the right way to write about such matters.
3. He is just that sort of man. They are all unconscious clichés, and either
 (a) He is a bad writer with a poor stock of phrases, but perfectly intelligent, or
 (b) He is a pompous twit.

Again, I must leave the reader to decide for himself which is the right answer. The charitable reader will go for a combination of (2) and (3a). In that case it might be better to think in terms less of clothes or faces than of mannerisms, or gestures. Phrases like the ones used above are just awkward habits, or gaucheries, such as one might find in a man who is always scratching his ear, or has a nervous cough, or waves his hands too much when he is talking. Personally (I must make it clear that I know nothing about the author) I find them offensive, the linguistic equivalent of a man picking his nose or breaking wind in public.

Though highly objectionable, they are relatively harmless. Here is another example:

> In the past few months the residents' committee have sought my assistance in stimulating an awareness of wider community problems in their district.[18]

Not much harm in this. 'Sought my assistance' and 'stimulating an awareness' are just verbal nosepickings.

In fact most of the clichés, or supposed clichés (depending on who is doing the supposing) which have been dealt with so far in this book are of a kind which does little harm to anyone; many, as I have tried to show, are positively useful, if not beneficial. Obvious exceptions are the example of Unesco-speak given a few pages earlier, and the more heavily-loaded clichés to be found in some of the 'stories' in the Tory gutter Press (miners' pickets do not shout, they 'howl', and so on). But there is also a whole class of vicious clichés.

Clichés are vicious either when they betray a dangerous absence of thought in those who use them, or when they are intended to prevent thought in those who hear them or read them. The most vicious form of all is the slogan-cliché.

The expert on slogan-clichés was, of course, George Orwell. The 'B Vocabulary' of Newspeak was really a carefully-refined slogan vocabulary, specifically designed 'to make speech, and especially speech on any subject not ideologically neutral, as near as possible independent of consciousness', rousing 'the minimum of echoes in the speaker's mind' and 'intended to impose a desirable mental attitude upon the person using them'.[19] Current Western political jargon is not so sinister – Orwell did not say it would become so, only that it might, if we were not careful – but it can certainly induce a dangerous state of unthought in those who transmit it or receive it.

Here are a few of the commoner examples of words or phrases which can easily be used by those who like talking with their minds shut: middle-class values; ordinary working people; profit motive; bourgeois mentality; capitalist conspiracy; class legislation; workers' struggle; workers' solidarity; imperialist aggression; smash; fascist; obscene.

Those are from the Left. From the Right we have: middle-class values; ordinary working people; profit motive; man in the street; centres of excellence; price of freedom; spirit of private enterprise; spirit of the nation; the little man; demands of the market place; maintenance of standards; finest traditions; obscene.[20]

The fact that four of them come in both lists suggests that, used just like that, they are pretty low on content. Middle-class values are good or bad, depending on what you think they are. 'The ordinary working people' are credited with whatever sentiments coincide with those of the political party being spoken for. 'Obscene' is a word more often heard on the Left than on the Right, but can be taken to refer to anything with which the speaker's party happens violently to disagree. To expressions common to both ways of thinking can be added 'caring community', 'dictates of natural justice', and the word 'exploit'. There is a great deal of 'exploitation' in a political speaker's vocabulary. The big multinational conglomerates undoubtedly exploit the working man, but the big union bosses exploit him too. Most of all, one might add, political speakers exploit their audiences.[21]

There is also a moderately-sized list of Left-wing clichés, including a number of *isms* – revisionism, entryism, deviationism – which do not come in here, though they are sometimes used as handy blunt instruments with which to belabour opponents, mostly within the movement. These specialised clichés should properly be put under the heading of jargon, which is not the subject of this book.

It is easy, when considering clichés, to stray into the subject of jargon on the one side, and idioms on the other. (More about idioms in the next chapter.) Each has a bearing on clichés. Idioms, like clichés, can tell us quite a bit about the person who is using them; and jargon can bring comfort to those who share it.

Those who do venture into the wide field of jargon are fond of attempting a distinction between 'necessary' and 'unnecessary' jargon, that is, between expressions which are merely obscurantist, and expressions which have no accurate substitute in ordinary speech. But one has to ask, necessary to whom? 'Unnecessary' jargon can, after all, be a splendid tonic for those among whom it is exchanged. Children, too, have their secret language, and we do not discourage them.

I cannot resist ending this chapter, however, with a grand example of adult jargon.

> After refusing to allow for a moment that there can be any inconsistency between *Strictness* and *Economy*, and asserting that they are parallel, [Professor Androutsos] proceeds further to consider typical primitive cases of the disposition of Economy, such as the reception of Donatists, Demi-Arians, and Nestorians, and particularly the action of St Basil who, on account of 'an Economy of many things', received the followers of Zoius and Satorninus but forbade

the Nicopolitans to receive ordination from Phronton, of Athanasius who rejected the originators of heresies but who accepted in their orders those carried away by force or necessity, of Cyril of Alexandria, who urged Gennadius not to avoid Communion with Proclus 'on account of the economies of the case', 'which at times must be strained a little beyond what is necessary', of the Third Ecumenical Council which accepted the Messalian clergy in their Orders, and of the Seventh Ecumenical Council which declared that clergy who renounce their heresy are to be received in their Orders.[22]

Nothing wrong with this sentence. The specialised uses of the words 'strictness' and 'economy' have already been explained by the charming and scholarly author, and anyone with enough initial interest to want to read the book will probably know who the Demi-Arians were. This is jargon in the right place.

8 · Orwell and Partridge

If clichés are to be deplored, it is for any of three reasons. First, if they fail to convey the intended message to those they are aimed at. Second, if they offend against taste, or are in other ways offensive. Third, if they are either self-deceptive, or designed to deceive others. It was the third kind which most alarmed Orwell in his essay on 'Politics and the English Language' of 1946. He is not interested in what he calls 'the literary use of language' – whatever that means (what is the difference between a 'literary' statement and another written statement?) – but merely with 'language as an instrument for expressing and not for concealing or preventing thought'.

Political language, he says, 'is designed to make lies sound truthful, and murder respectable, and to give an appearance of solidity to pure wind.'[1] And unless we 'let the meaning choose the word, and not the other way about', we are all at risk from the politicians, because we will begin to think sloppily ourselves, and are in danger of stopping thinking altogether.

His recipe for preventing this is drastic indeed. Concrete rather than abstract terms; active verbs, rather than passive ones; a ruthless cutting out of words that are not needed. His first two rules are:

1. Never use a metaphor, simile or other figure of speech which you are used to seeing in print.
2. Never use a long word where a short one will do.[2]

Orwell's advice has had a big influence on writers over the past three decades or so. His remark about figures of speech which people are 'used to seeing in print' is very much like that of the sub-editor on the old *News Chronicle* whom I quoted earlier ('You can bet your boots it's a cliché'). Its effect, if the advice is carefully followed, can be inhibiting, and in two ways.

First, it can inhibit the speaker or writer. Orwell says that a scrupulous writer will always ask himself what he is trying to say before he starts writing, then look for words which will help him make his meaning clearer. This in itself is perfectly sound advice, and is always being given to young writers, but it betrays a naïve view of what 'meaning' is. For 'meaning' cannot be bought by the kilo. Unless we are talking in purely functional English ('Put the meat in the freezer'), our statements nearly always carry with them some conscious or unconscious attitude towards the thing we are writing about or talking about. A value of some sort is being applied to what is being described. This is true not only in the case of simple opinions – 'So-and-so is a nice man' – but in situations where the thing may seem simple, but the speaker's attitude to it is not.

For example, we can say: 'Henry is getting married.' That is describing something, according to the Orwell formula, in the shortest and simplest way. But it says nothing about what we think of Henry or his marriage. If the words are spoken, a gesture (a casting of the eyes towards the ceiling, perhaps) might convey it. If they are written, then there is a large store of phrases at our disposal, which are far more informative than the simple statement. Henry is tying the knot, he is taking the plunge, he is going legal, he's going into double harness, he is about to enjoy connubial bliss. Marriage is a match, an alliance, a union, the state of holy matrimony. Many of these phrases are common enough for people to be 'used to seeing them', many are the most ordinary of clichés. (For yet more, see Roget's *Thesaurus*, that treasure-house of them.) Each one of them conveys an attitude. Each one tells the reader or listener more – carries more 'meaning', in fact – than the bare remark. It is wrong to suppose that the crisper or shorter way of putting something is more informative than the wordier, more roundabout way.

And if the wordier way is also familiar to the person reading the remark, so much the better. Most of those cited above imply some degree of cynicism, except, perhaps, the last two. But each carries its own nuance. The less familiar the term used, the less easily will the exact nuance be taken up. For of course the second way in which Orwell's advice is inhibiting is in its effect, if it is followed, on the readers or listeners. On the really interesting points – is it a good match, does the writer think Henry will be happy, and so forth – they are left in the dark.

This is perhaps why one gets upset when Orwell tries to claim an undefined distinction between 'literary' and other writing, as though poetry and fiction were all in the mind, but other kinds of writing were, so to speak, somewhere else. In fact 'non-literary' writing, if one must use the word, can be infinitely subtle. All those different ways of passing on the news of a man's impending marriage mean something slightly different from each other. This is why Roget's *Thesaurus* is such an unsatisfactory place in which to look up synonyms. How often has one heard frustrated people saying they are looking for 'another word for such-and-such' and not finding it in Roget! Of course they can't find it, because Roget is not a synonym dictionary. Peter Mark Roget made this clear in his preface to the original edition. 'The assistance it gives', he wrote,

> is that of furnishing on every topic a copious store of words and phrases, adapted to express *all the recognisable shades and modifications of the general idea*

under which they are arranged. (My italics.)[3] Any publisher who, Roget being out of copyright, brings out a synonym dictionary based on the *Thesaurus*, with his name on the spine (it has happened), ought to be had up under the Trade Descriptions Act.

Many of the unconscious clichés ridiculed by Orwell are bursting with more or less subtle meaning. He complains that modern writing at its worst

> does not consist in picking out words for the sake of their meaning and inventing images in order to make the meaning clearer. It consists of gumming together long strips of words which have already been set in order by someone else.[4]

That, of course, was exactly the formula recommended by Roger Ascham in the sixteenth century to those who wanted to learn how to write good prose. First you see what others have done, and try to emulate them; then, and only then, do you fly solo. Orwell himself was an accomplished solo flier and his work is full of marvellous original images, many of them in the form of similes; but we can't all be Orwells.

However, the unconscious clichés I am thinking of here are of a humbler sort, a long way away from either Orwell's brilliance or the rhetoric of the Elizabethan schoolmen. Orwell hates the 'pretentious, Latinised style' which produces tags such as *consideration which we would do well to bear in mind* and *a conclusion to which we would all readily assent*. These are really just habits of speech. They are not attractive, indeed they can be deeply tedious. I have already labelled this sort of cliché the 'nosepicking cliché' because of what it tells us about the character of the person using it. But it should not be confused with the viciousness which makes politicians talk about liberating a city when they mean that they have destroyed it, or stabilising a population when they mean they have massacred half the citizens.

If, in order to avoid the major hypocrisies, we try to avoid elaboration of any sort, we shall end up the poorer. It is quite wrong to think that the Anglo-Saxon or Middle English word is always better than the Latin- or Greek-derived word. A small example: Neil Kinnock, the Opposition leader, was quoted on 1 August 1984 as having said: 'Naturally I have been gratified by some of the kindly words said about me.' To follow Orwell's advice he should have said 'pleased'. But 'pleased' would have suggested something quite different from 'gratified'. 'Gratified' is much cooler; one can acquire gratification from a good cigar.[5]

None of this is to belittle Orwell's campaign for honesty in politics. My point is that we must *distinguish*. To say that certain sorts of writing are 'good' and others 'bad', without examining the 'goodness' or 'badness', is to fall into just that state of unthinkingness that Orwell himself was fighting against.

This, it seems to me, is much what the late Eric Partridge did when he compiled his *A Dictionary of Clichés*. (The 'A' simply means that he couldn't think of all of them.) When he wrote in his introduction that their ubiquity was rather frightening, at first I thought he merely meant he was daunted by the task he had set himself. 'To collect clichés is not an easy job,' he writes in his preface. In his preface to the fifth edition, however, he makes it clear that he is serious. 'The situation seems to have become worse,' he writes, lamenting 'the persistence of these well-worn substitutes for thinking'.

But to compile a dictionary of clichés is in itself an act of thoughtlessness. When is a cliché not a cliché? At what stage does Partridge, or anyone else, decide that a word or phrase has got to the stage in its career at which it qualifies for being so labelled?

It is impossible to make a simple, arbitrary distinction between a cliché and a not-cliché. To try to do so is as pointless as it is to compile one of those lists which appear from time to time in one or another of the Sunday colour supplements: 'Who's In, Who's Out'. In: David Owen, Princess Anne. Out: A. N. Wilson, Elton John. Explanation? None.

Some phrases are a little over-used, others need to be regarded with care, others again are on the way to becoming fully-grown self-defeating soporifics. The last category is, of course, by far the least interesting, so there is little point in making a list of them, though even they, in the hands of a man like P. G. Wodehouse, can once again be made to give pleasure.

Partridge's dictionary makes no effort to chart the rake's progress of a cliché, no effort to evaluate its strength, or whatever strength it has left. He categorises clichés into various sorts – fly-blown phrases, pointless metaphors and so forth – without reflecting on what one would have thought should be the really interesting questions to be asked of any one of them: what is in the mind of the person who offers it, and what is the effect on the people who are on the receiving end of it? What (to use the cant term) is the nature of the transaction?

Why are clichés in the *Express* different from those in the *Guardian*? Why would a *Guardian* cliché not even *be* a cliché in the *Express*? And, for that, matter, *vice versa*?

Perhaps one is asking too much of him here; there is evidence that Partridge, an extraordinarily mercurial man, got this one up in something of a hurry – it was just another of his busy magpie activities among the bric-á-brac of language. But his attempt to classify language as cliché (bad), and some other unrecorded thing which can be presumed to be original (good), was surely begging a thousand questions. Anyway, it chimed in with the way people had been taught to think about language, and has done very well ever since it first appeared in 1940. It has hardly been out of print, and has sold something over 10,000 copies since it went into paperback in 1978.

In the preface to the paperback edition Partridge noted with approval that it would now be more accessible to teachers and students, which surprised me a bit, because before that I had thought of it simply as a *jeu d'esprit*, but it appears that Partridge, as I say, really took his own nonsense seriously. In that case, it is the longest list of what Fleet Street style-book editors call Barred Expressions that has ever been compiled.

Partridge divides his list into four broad, overlapping categories, all of them by implication 'bad'. They are:

1. *Idioms that have become clichés.* That is, those that have been 'so indiscriminately used that the original point has been blunted or even removed entirely'.
2. *Other hackneyed phrases.* That is, those that are 'so hackneyed as to be knock-kneed and spavined'. [A carriage-trade pun.]
3. *Stock phrases from foreign languages.*
4. *Stock phrases from English literature.*

The first two take up about four-fifths of the whole. In the first, there seems on the face of it to be a confusion between idioms and metaphors. Here Partridge misses a point which was clear to George Orwell. English is an exceptionally metaphorical language: it is taking on new metaphors all the time, and absorbing them into the general vocabulary. And a metaphor goes through three phases.

During the first phase the analogy is absolutely clear to everyone. When people said they proposed to shed light on a subject the immediate image presented itself of someone opening the flap of a lantern and allowing it to emit a beam. In the second phase the image becomes rather boring – once so evocative, it no longer stirs the mind. In the third phase the original metaphorical content has been more or less forgotten (particularly, in this case, since the invention of the electric switch). What had been a cliché has come through the barrier, as it were, and is no longer such, but simply a part of the language. It has become, in short, an idiom.

Other metaphors and similes are so startling or clever that they are taken up by everyone and used so often that they arrive at the second phase almost immediately. Bright comparisons involving vicarage garden parties and snowballs in hell could never have lasted long. These are the 'instant clichés'.

But Partridge's big first category of clichés – those whose point has been blunted or removed entirely, as he puts it – takes no account of these processes. The metaphor whose point has been entirely removed might well have 'come through the barrier' and therefore be quite acceptable as an idiomatic phrase. Clichés about snowballs in hell, on the other hand, are unlikely to lose their point: whether we believe in hell or not, we go on knowing that it is supposed to be a place of eternal fire. We tire of them the sooner for it. It is the metaphor whose meaning *has* been lost that is likely to survive. (Orwell makes the same point when he says that a metaphor which is technically 'dead' has 'in effect reverted to being an ordinary word and can generally be used without loss of vividness'. For Orwell, vivid = new.) So Partridge got it the wrong way round.[6]

His second category ('Other hackneyed phrases') is a ragbag of many different sorts of cliché. It is in his last two sections that he really unfurls his colours. He makes the amazing claim that some English quotations are clichés only when they are misquoted. What he means is that the misquotations are more frequent than the correct versions: therefore, because they are often used, they *must* be clichés. I hope I have said enough already to make it clear that the age of a phrase does not necessarily bear any relation to the strength of its impact. But Partridge also reveals that he is a snob. He dislikes that use of foreign phrases and Latin tags which come from 'love of display' (a gentleman, one infers, should never be conspicuous). Misquotations upset him dreadfully, and so does 'a half-education – that snare of the half-baked and the ready-made'. So 'an uncultured, little-reading person sees a stock phrase and thinks it apt and smart; he forgets that its aptness should put him on his guard'. In other words, kindly get off the pavement. Only cultured persons should attempt to quote great authors.

Again, politicians use clichés, he says, because they address large audiences 'on the majority of whose individual members subtlety and style would be wasted'. At the same time he is alarmed by their increasing use by the middle and upper classes, who presumably ought to know better. He is, shall we say, a man of taste. A cliché is something which offends *his*. He does, however, at one point offer what looks after all like a pretty sensible definition:

> A cliché is an outworn phrase, or short sentence, that has become so hackneyed that careful speakers and scrupulous writers avoid it because they feel that its use is an insult to the intelligence of their audience or public.

That really is getting us somewhere, since it actually takes account of the context. But his classification still seems to me to be absurdly inadequate.

A much better way of doing it, I should have thought, would be to say that *familiar words and phrases* fall roughly into the following classes:

1. *Vicious.* Designed to deceive the public. Used by dictators (all the time), politicians (some of the time), captains of industry. (*Shake-out* and *slimming down* sound good to the shareholders, bad to the sacked employees.)
2. *Euphemistic.* Overlaps with the above. *Pass on* for *die*; *not quite himself* for *drunk*. Used by undertakers, bank managers, business men in general (*Your early reply would be*

appreciated). Also, depending on whom we are with, by you and me.

3. *Self-deluding.* Overlaps with both of the above. Also used by people who have risen to positions which are a bit too much for them (in other words, people who have demonstrated the Peter Principle). Used by many teachers, lecturers and 'educationists', among others, who have been taken in by their own vocabulary, and genuinely think that if they write *teacher-pupil interface* or *open-ended perspective* or *hierarchical structure* they have said something profound.

4. *Plain ugly.* Phrases which are pretty harmless in themselves but show some more or less unpleasant lapse of taste. Range from the simple phrase used in the public bar (too vulgar to mention here) to the pseudo-literary quip (*arms of Morpheus* for *sleep*) and other facetious circumlocutions in the wrong context (*Sorry to hear your son has turned up his toes*), to irritating idioms *(If I may venture an opinion)*. The 'nosepicking' cliché.

5. *Instant.* Overlaps with the category immediately above. Phrases that are so vivid (*cat on hot bricks*; *walking on eggs*; *over the moon*) that they can't last. They are still used, but are so tired that they are hardly acceptable anywhere but in speech.

Those are the nasty ones, more or less in descending order of nastiness. The vice-free ones are harder to classify, but one can easily identify:

6. *Ironic, or camp.* Everyone knows them – and loves them. Used so as to strengthen an acquaintanceship; or with an unspoken apology for them; or simply for the pleasure of them. An enormous category. (See Chapter Four.) Partridge does very occasionally write 'ironic' against one of his examples.

7. *Phrases that have come through the cliché-barrier.* (*Shed light, deliver the goods, keep at arm's length, wash one's hands of,* etc.) These are idioms which have become absorbed into the

language and have no special flavour. Another very big category.
8. *Idiomatic doublets.* Nothing wrong or vicious about these. (*Rack and ruin, simply and solely, safe and sound, fits and starts, leaps and bounds,* etc.) Some are more effective than others. The weaker ones are usually an adjective-noun or adverb-adjective combination, which can have the curious effect of weakening the impact of what is said, instead of intensifying it. (*Blissful ignorance, bitter complaint, desperately unhappy.*) A person who is described as *totally useless* is no more useless than a person who is merely *useless. Terror* is not much worse for being called *abject.*
9. *Modified catchphrases.* Old favourites given a quick jab of rejuvenating fluid. (*Pain in the knee* for *neck,* etc., etc.)

Partridge shovels all these different kinds into his dictionary, without any distinction whatever, except that he does every now and then put an asterisk against an entry, to show that it is 'particularly hackneyed' or otherwise objectionable, in his view of the thing.

I have not counted all his examples, but I suppose they come to something between 2,000 and 3,000. I took a sample of 373 (the letters 'B' and 'S'). Between 50 and 60 of these are obsolete (*balm in Gilead, barmecide feast,* etc.), largely because fewer people nowadays read the Bible, or the Arabian Nights, or whatever. Many of them have a Flaubertian flavour – not in the sense that Partridge copied Flaubert, which he did not, but that they are the kind of rather pretentious thing Flaubert would have been amused by. Roughly another 80 are in my view not really hackneyed phrases but often-used idioms *(stage whisper, steal someone's thunder, stay the course,* etc., etc.). Partridge even includes phrases like *smack's one's lips, sooner or later, in the same boat, before you know where you are,* and others which have either long since 'broken the barrier' or become part of common speech; to forbid their use would be to wipe out whole tracts of the English language.

That leaves some 240, or just under two-thirds of my sample. Of these, I reckon that 140 or so really are tired old warhorses which should be pensioned off (*birds of a feather, blot on the landscape, bone of contention*), though some of them can still be used in conversation without fear of offence; in writing, any but the most permissive of editors would want to strike them out.

The remaining hundred can be divided equally between what might be called aggregations – clumps of words which have a natural attraction for each other, such as *bow and scrape, blissful ignorance, steady improvement, stress and strain, strictly accurate* and so forth – and circumlocutions. The circumlocutions can be either of the lowest sort (*stew in your own juice*) or the high-flown or 'literary' (*still small voice, bird of ill omen*). As I have shown earlier, these devices have an ancient ancestry. When circumlocutions appear in the old sagas they are called kennings and everyone says how splendid they are. Partridge takes a different view of them. He writes:

> Poets have found the literate, the cultured cliché (rosy-fingered dawn) invaluable for the eking-out of the metric and the conquest of the evasive rhyme; a convenient faute de mieux.[7]

This must be the ineptest thing he ever said. 'Rosy-fingered dawn' was already a cliché (in the Partridge sense of a phrase which has been used a lot) in Homer's day. If we were to take Partridge at his word, we would have to junk half the poetry ever written.

Whether one regards the phrases in these last two categories – the doublets and the circumlocutions – as pensionable, or as still having work to do, is purely a matter of taste and circumstance.

Let us take a few words consecutively listed by Partridge, not in the main body of the dictionary, but in the introduction, where he is explaining his classifications. Under his second heading – phrases which are 'knock-kneed and spavined' – and its first ('general') sub-heading, he names as examples (to start at random) the following expressions, to each of which I attach a purely personal view of my own. Others may feel differently about them.

Generous to a fault. A mindless word-pairing now, to be avoided.
Glorious victory. This has been a well-known camp expression for (I guess) at least a hundred years (compare the 'famous victory' which puzzled Little Peterkin) and still has its uses in satire. Ridiculous to bracket it with the above.
Golden mean. Obsolete. Starred by Partridge, as being particularly objectionable; but note his intense dislike of Latin tags, unless used by cultured people. Fell out of use when even cultured people stopped reading Horace.
Good Queen Bess. Obsolete.
Grievous error. Automatic pairing. A grievous error is no worse than a bad error.
Grow no younger. Unpleasing euphemistic circumlocution (my class 2).
Halcyon days. Starred by Partridge because he doesn't like classical allusions getting into the hands of the common people. Obsolescent now anyway.
Here today and gone tomorrow. I see no objection to this little-used phrase.
Hearty British cheer. Obsolete or ironic.
Highly improbable. This is such a closely-welded pairing that it almost qualifies as an idiom. Test: if you take away 'highly' and substitute 'very' it doesn't sound any better, only a little quaint, as though a foreigner were talking. (Try saying 'spill the peas' and see if anyone understands you, to use an extreme example.)
Hobson's choice. Obsolete, or nearly. Had a surprisingly long

run. No one really knows its origin, as Partridge points out.
Imagination runs riot. 'Camp'.
Kindred spirit. I can see no objection to this harmless piece of periphrasis.
Known for a fact. 'Nosepicker'.
Last but not least. Confined to bad after-dinner speakers, putting votes of thanks. Generally greeted with sighs of relief.
Mine host. Unobjectionable pub cliché, semi-ironic.
Miraculous escape. A newspaper pairing. See Chapter Six.
Moot point. Partridge stars this, as one would expect: hardly anyone knows what it means any more, and he dislikes people using metaphors of which they do not know the origin. If you do not share this view, *moot point* becomes acceptable.
Nip in the bud. Also starred, perhaps for the same reason. Personally, I should have thought it had very nearly gone 'through the barrier'. (Test: Would you use it yourself? Well, probably not . . .)
Of a certain age. Still a useful periphrasis.
The open road. Interesting history. Originally applied to walking (Partridge cites E. V. Lucas's book of that title, which appeared in 1899), then to motoring (the Austin company actually marketed a model called the 'Open Road Tourer' in about 1930), now, since roads are pleasant places neither for walkers nor for motorists, used only with deep irony. Partridge includes it because it was very popular early in the century. (He does not refer to its application to motoring.) Partridge dislikes anything which is popular. Very perverse.
A picture of health. Dead in writing. Still available for 'camp' or bantering purposes.
Psychological moment. Dreadful. Brings a rush of sympathy for all Partridge has been saying about people using expressions they don't understand.
Quite the opposite. What is wrong with this?
Runs in the blood. Or this?

Salt of the earth. 'Camp' in writing. Serious in conversation.
Scantily clad. Was this ever used seriously? I suspect Partridge would class it as a vulgarism. I would be inclined to put it in my own category 4.
Second to none; sick at heart; soul of honour. I applaud E.P.'s inclusion of all these three, and share his distaste for them, though he has starred none of them. This is, again, a matter of taste. I just don't think (to generalise) that I would much warm to anyone who used them. Significantly, all are to do with sentiment – the trickiest area.
Staff of life. Ghastly circumlocution.
Superhuman effort. Not much effort needed to avoid this. An automatic doublet.
Terminated fatally. Another newspaper phrase; again, see Chapter Six. Also my class 2.
Venture an opinion. A real 'nosepicker'! (Ugh.)
The why and the wherefore. Almost as bad.
You could have knocked me down with a feather. 'Instant' cliché.

The above represent only my own views of the examples given; other people, as I say, may think differently about each one of them. But on my count, only about half of them could really be called objectionable, in whatever circumstances one heard or read them. Yet Partridge almost certainly picked them out for his introduction as notably 'bad' examples. A randomly-chosen couple of pages from the Dictionary itself might show a different proportion:

Hold one's own. An idiom.
Hole-and-corner. Ditto.
Holiday exodus. Newspaper cliché once, but not common enough nowadays to merit the term.
Hollow tones. I don't know why P. included this. He does not have 'rings hollow' which I would have thought was a more likely target for him.

Holy matrimony. 'Used seriously and correctly, it is obviously not a cliché.' Therefore presumably must not be used facetiously. This is a matter of taste. But I cannot, in general, see why it is 'wrong' to make use of a term from the Prayer Book outside its context. It's just part of the available culture.

Home comforts. Hardly a cliché? P. classes it as 'borderline case of incipient cliché'.

Home of lost causes. Starred by Partridge, presumably for reasons already discussed. If I came across it in a piece of copy I was sub-editing, I would be tempted to cross it out, or suggest to author that he or she should do so.

Home of one's own. Think of a better way of putting it, if there is one!

Homeric laughter. Cf. Flaubert. Obsolete.

To turn an honest penny. Still available in my class 6.

The honest truth. Very low grade. Spoken only.

Hope against hope. Starred by P., I am not sure why. Really an idiom by now, but admittedly not a very attractive one.

Hope deferred. (Short for 'Hope deferred maketh the heart sick.') Obsolete.

Hope springs eternal. Here at last is a fully-paid-up, absolutely genuine cliché. (Originally, of course, from Pope's *Essay on Man*.) Could hardly be used without shame even in semi-facetious conversations as discussed in Chapter Four.

Hopeless despair. I did not know this as a cliché. It's just a worthless pleonasm, I should have thought.

Horse of another colour. Surely this quaint metaphor, dating at least as far back as Shakespeare, but apparently, according to P., becoming a cliché in about 1860, is obsolete now; or, if it *is* used, rare enough not to be thought of as a 'cliché'.

To have a host of friends. Very low grade.

Hotly contested. A harmless pairing, almost idiomatic. Why try to proscribe it?

In one's hour of need. Mostly 'camp'.
House and home. Another harmless pairing, though by now somewhat quaint in writing; OK in conversation.
Tell me how the world wags. Shakespearean. Obsolete.

These, from one double-page spread of Partridge's Dictionary (pages 108–9), come by chance to the same number as my earlier sample from his introduction – 21. But this time only four of them seem to me to be objectionable, and another four at least are obsolete; and looking at one or two of the others one wonders why they are there. The pages were chosen quite at random and I doubt if they differ much from the general pattern. In my sample from 'B' and 'S' I reckoned that about one in three was a 'tired old war horse' (but some could still be used in conversation). In the sample above only one in five is objectionable, though one or two others are getting pretty tired.

Anyway, Partridge did not compile his Dictionary with a view to statistical analysis, and he himself admits in his introduction that the whole thing is pretty subjective. At the same time he deplores clichés and says that their ubiquity is alarming. Thus do nervous horses shy at leaves, not being sure what they are.

What I find worrying, myself, is not that clichés are so ubiquitous, whatever they may be, but that Partridge and others have trained so many of us to beware of anything which *might* be called one, thus inhibiting our means of self-expression. Sir Ernest Gowers, whose *Plain Words* first came out in 1948, has been almost as influential as Partridge here – perhaps even more influential. His advice to those who want to write good English is not very different from Orwell's, though it is more permissive. Citing H. W. Fowler and Sir Arthur Quiller-Couch in support, he offers these rules:

> Use no more words than are necessary to express your meaning, for if you use more you are likely to obscure it and to tire your reader. In particular do not use superfluous adjectives and adverbs and do not use roundabout phrases where single words would serve.
>
> Use familiar words rather than the far-fetched, if they express your meaning equally well; for the familiar are more likely to be readily understood.
>
> Use words with a precise meaning rather than those that are vague . . . and in particular prefer concrete words to abstract, for they are more likely to have a precise meaning.[8]

Gowers writes with great elegance himself and his book had a huge success. He is particularly good at laughing people out of bad habits, like the use of what he calls 'dressing-gown adverbs', as though certain adjectives, such as 'short', 'long', 'many', 'few', etc., 'were naked and must hastily have an adverbial dressing gown thrown around them', such as 'unduly', 'relatively' and 'comparatively'. And he is splendid on ineptly-applied metaphors, among them 'ceiling' and 'target'. Also 'breakdown'.

Thus:

> Unfortunately a breakdown of British trade is not possible

and

> In determining the floor space, a ceiling of 15,000 square feet should normally be the limit

and

> Headline: 'Export Target Hit'. (Which meant it was not hit.)

But people forgot that Gowers had a particular aim: to help civil servants communicate with those whom they impersonally thought of as 'the public'; to get them to be more human, and to write in 'the real language of men'. Clarity and simplicity were needed, not nuances. Since he was not after subtlety, his rules for good writing are quite adequate. They would not be adequate for a broader exchange of ideas, where subtlety and ambivalence are often not only inevitable but even, sometimes, actually necessary. And the rules certainly would not do for transmitting feelings.

In a section on clichés themselves, Gowers offers the best definition so far:

> A phrase whose aptness in a particular context when it was first invented has won it such popularity that it has become hackneyed, and is used without thought in contexts where it is no longer apt.[9]

He has taken the point later to be made at greater length by Randolph Quirk, that the crucial thing is the context. 'A cliché ... is a bad thing, not to be employed by self-respecting writers,' he says. He then names a number of expressions which *in all circumstances* should be regarded as clichés, and adds:

> But a vast number of other expressions may or may not be clichés. It depends on whether they are used unthinkingly as reach-me-downs or deliberately chosen as the best means of saying what the writer wants to say.

Here we are back with the idea of language as clothing. Richard Hoggard wrote about 'verbal morning dress', and Gowers himself about 'dressing-gown adverbs'. We often think of a cliché as a 'ready-made phrase'; and here is Gowers again writing about 'reach-me-downs'. The analogy is useful.

To take it further, one can imagine a man in a hurry buying a suit off the peg; he knows it doesn't fit him perfectly but it is all he has time to get. Another man (well, most of us in fact) hasn't enough money for anything else, or, to translate the analogy back into terms of language, he has a poor stock of words, or perhaps he merely has a not particularly original mind. Gowers mentions a number of clichés listed by Partridge and says that if a writer chooses them because he or she knows them to be the aptest for the occasion, then they are *not* clichés (they include 'swing of the pendulum', *'sui generis'* and 'white elephant'). But, as I say, a choice is not always available. One might take a phrase off the peg knowing quite well that it is not a perfect fit and that it is being used by other people all over the place, but one simply doesn't have the means to find another. A vast number of expressions are being used all the time in just these circumstances.

The 'fitness for purpose' argument does not always work: it is not enough to say that if a person deliberately chooses a phrase that fits his meaning, this must necessarily excuse him from having committed a cliché. The best vehicle for an old idea may be an old phrase. The person who uses the expression 'durance vile' (in all circumstances a cliché, according to Gowers) may be the sort of person who really does think of imprisonment in just that slightly jokey way. We may not like him very much for it, but this does not mean that he has failed to say what he set out to say.

The OED Supplement cited as one of its examples of the word (used as an adjective this time) an article in the *Listener* of 30 July 1959, which spoke of 'the kind of fond reminiscence which comes too near the cliché view of human situations'. What did it mean? I looked the article up. The writer, Ian Rodger, was reviewing a radio play by Bernard Kops called *The Street Game* which, said Mr Rodger, was 'sticky with rather too much sentiment and . . . glued together with some music by Mr Alexander Goehr . . . Mr Kops showed signs in his last work of becoming more objective but he moved back on this occasion to the kind of fond reminiscence which comes too near the cliché view', etc.

In other words Mr Kops was too schmaltzy for Mr Rodger. The play was semi-autobiographical and the critic was saying that the playwright wasn't seeing his own past straight; he was not being 'objective'. Unless the two shared their childhoods, though, the best judge of the play's truth was surely Mr Kops, whose sentiments may have exactly matched the way it was, for all we know. So what is a 'cliché view' in this case? Mr Rodger uses it in the sense of 'an inaccurate view', but if he had been using the word in its proper sense of 'hackneyed', he would have meant merely that Mr Kops was telling us about things we had heard much too often before, so that we were bored.

To say, therefore, with Gowers that a cliché ceases to be a cliché if it expresses what the writer wants to convey will not really meet the case, and the *Listener* example confuses the issue. Here is another example of the same sort, from *The Times* of 26 July 1983:

> Little, other than love, gives the majority of West Indians, of any colour and creed, the same unqualified delight as listening, in the streets or on the beaches or outside the rum shops or as they cut cane, to a West Indian victory at Sydney or Lord's.

That was by the newspaper's cricket correspondent, John Woodcock, writing from London. There is no doubt that Mr Woodcock said exactly what he wanted to say. Indeed, he could hardly have put it better. It fully meets Gowers's requirement of precision. We have here a perfect expression of what anyone who has never been to the West Indies thinks they must be like, complete with love, rum, a sunny open-air life, the cane harvest and an obsession with cricket. In fact it fits so well with the conventional view that we can't help suspecting that it must be wrong. On the other hand it could very well be absolutely right, in two senses. It could show what the West Indies are in fact like, but that is a matter of opinion. More important, it could accord with what Mr Woodcock found when he went there himself. In that case, we can hardly blame him for setting down what he thought he saw. If we are to go along with Sir Ernest Gowers, we will have to say that a cliché view is not the same as a cliché.

What is wrong with Mr Woodcock's idea of the West Indies (assuming – sudden thought – that he wasn't pulling our legs) is the same as what was wrong with A. C. Benson's cosy description of his life at Magdalene or Hugh Walpole's equally cosy description of a cathedral town. We are in the happy world of tosh. The water-colourist Barbara Jones, in her book of advice to amateurs published in 1960,[10] ends with some interesting tips on how to avoid the same kind of thing in painting. She suggests that if you give an intelligent friend pencil and paper and ask him or her to draw a ship, a beehive, an aeroplane and a plough, they will probably produce a galleon, a straw skep, a biplane and an Anglo-Saxon agricultural implement. If they draw a garden it will be infested with hollyhocks, crazy paving, an old well, a pergola and a sundial, whatever their own garden looks like. Barbara Jones goes on:

> You want only to be able to paint graceful little lyrical water-colours with Corfe Castle rather mauve on the horizon? Perhaps you will be able to do this and rest content, but not if you think.

And she points out that the great English landscape painters like Girtin, Cotman and the rest always put in the unromantic bits, 'unscientifically farmed fields, carter's wains, drunken soldiers, muddy roads, unrestored churches'. In the end, she says, it must always be 'the painter's own eye and mind. Your eye and your mind' that matters. This was exactly what Messrs Stratta, Dixon and Wilkinson wanted from the teachers on their courses, and exactly what prompted one of those teachers to write:

> I wanted to choose a picture which would relate more closely to my experience. This was the first difficulty. What kind of picture should I choose – so that I may identify with it – *my* emotions, *my* thoughts, *my* experiences?

And 'their key words, rather than ours' was what Ken Worpole wanted from his pupils. But see where it gets us. Benson tries to put down on paper *his* experience when the sunlight struck a corner of the garden court, and I have no doubt that it was a genuine experience; Walpole, the self-confessed realist, does the same with his cathedral town, and John Woodcock tells the readers of his newspaper what *he* thinks of the West Indies. And what do we have? Tosh, just tosh.

So much for the Cult of Originality. The Cult of Originality assumes that we are all original – that if you ask people to produce something from out of their own heads the result will be different from what has already come out of other people's heads. We cannot all be Girtins and Cotmans; we cannot, as I say, all be Orwells.

The teacher just quoted above, who was trying to write about a city as he saw it, might have done a number of things. He might have seen the suburban tower-blocks as Triffids waiting to move into the centre, or as a workers' paradise *à la* Corbusier, or he might not have noticed them at all and seen only the cobbled streets of the old quarter. Whatever it was, he risked a 'cliché view', depending on who read the result. Mr Stratta might think the cobbles clichéd, while Mr Dixon or Mr Wilkinson might think the same of his tower-blocks. Poor man. The only inexcusable sin would have been to write about the Triffid-blocks if he had not actually seen them.

Let me return to where I began, with Ezra Pound. In the essay already quoted he divides writers – good writers, that is – into three sorts. First come the *masters*, who

> apart from their own inventions, are able to assimilate and co-ordinate a large number of preceding inventions ... They will either start with a core of their own and assimilate adjuncts, or they digest a vast mass of subject matter, apply a number of known modes of expression, and succeed in pervading the whole with some special quality of some special character of their own ...

Next come the *dilutes*, who produce 'some flabbier variant' of the above. Last come

> the men who do more or less good work in the more or less good style of a period.[11]

Most of us count ourselves lucky if we manage to squeeze into the third class, I should have thought. Why should the cliché-hunters keep on blaming us for not belonging to the second or first?

Those of us who listen too much to the cliché-hunters are putting ourselves in the same position (or a banausic equivalent of it) as T. S. Eliot deliberately put himself in when he wrote *The Cocktail Party*. As he explains in his famous lecture on *Poetry and Drama*,[12] he had felt that his previous plays, *Murder in the Cathedral* and *The Family Reunion*, had carried long sections in which the poetry got in the way, so to speak, of the action; such passages were 'too much like operatic arias'. So to avoid this he determined to lay down for himself

> the ascetic rule to avoid poetry which could not stand the test of dramatic utility: with such success, indeed, that it is

perhaps an open question whether there is any poetry in the play at all.

A poet who writes for the theatre, he says, must put his poetry 'on a very thin diet'. Eliot's self-denial here is a bit like Wordsworth's when he determined to ditch the poetic diction of his day: like Wordsworth, Eliot wanted 'to bring poetry into the world in which the audience lives': not to transport them into an artificial world, but to 'illuminate and transfigure' the world of every day. I have already mentioned the effect of this exercise in self-discipline on the worst of Wordsworth's verse. There is a parallel between this process and the position of an aspiring writer of today who, in his anxiety not to be accused of writing clichés, decides to junk all traditional expressions and literary allusions. He is, like Eliot, putting himself (or herself) on a very thin diet; unlike Eliot, he may find himself without the stamina to survive on it.

And of course a *general* move towards self-denial in these matters can be quite serious. It can lead to a literary equivalent of anorexia. Fay Weldon discusses the problem in her advice to an imaginary niece on how to write a novel.[13] Having mentioned Francis Thompson's *The Hound of Heaven* and the phrase in it, 'the arches of the years', she explains how 'we can't use this phrase now', partly because to do so would be 'plagiarism'; and anyway:

> It is the kind of thing writers used to depend on in their attempts to get taken seriously, and now we no longer can. We talk to an audience . . . and [to] a generation which has read so little it understands only the vernacular.

Mrs Weldon goes on to say that she doesn't think it matters much, and that writers just have to 'change and adapt'. (She means these words intransitively, I think: that is, writers must change themselves, not adapt other writers' work.) But again, we can't always be as strong as Mrs Weldon, when, having made it clear that 'the words a writer uses, even now, go back into a written history', she advises:

> The writer must summon his Idea out of nowhere, and his characters out of nothing.

(Nothing will come of nothing, as the old man said to Cordelia.) It is hard to share Mrs Weldon's unconcern at the prospect of 'a generation which has read so little it understands only the vernacular'. Why has it read so little? Is it, as I suspect, because teachers have for years now been telling pupils that what *they* think is what matters, and that therefore, by an extension of the argument, they can ignore what other people have thought and written in the past? The trouble is that this sort of process grows on itself. The East Sussex County Library, which I use, has a policy of weeding out from its various branches any books which in the judgment of its librarians 'no longer justify their place on the shelves', and of selling them or giving them away. I am not sure on what principle a book is deemed to be of no further use to the readers of East Sussex, but presumably one of the criteria must be the length of time that has passed since the book was last taken out. Libraries have to buy new books and of course shelf-space is limited. But the library also disperses its stock among all its branches, so that no reader has access to more than a limited sample of it. The rest is on microfiche catalogues, and the only readers likely to avail themselves of the microfiche are those who know what they are looking for; the others have to rely for their breadth of reading on what they see before them. At any rate, the condemned volumes are from time to time bundled into black plastic bags like those used by restaurants when they put out their excess trash for the dustman. Thousands of them are then laid out on trestle tables in a local secondary school. The policy may be right or it may be wrong, but I can only say that those corpse-like rows of books make a desperate sight.

Meanwhile, one surely can't help worrying about the cumulative effect of an education policy, spoken or unspoken, which undervalues what used to be a shared literary heritage, and the received wisdom which says that the successful writers are the ones who owe nothing to those who have gone before them. The process is the same as that seen in the disease of anorexia. The less the patients eat, the less they think they need. Meanwhile they get thinner . . .

9 · Some examples

In the end we are not much nearer a satisfactory definition of the cliché than we were at the beginning. I hope I have said enough to show why: why an agreed definition can never be possible, or even, dare I add, desirable. But I hope, too, that no one will think that I have been trying to defend the second-rate. I by no means defend it. I do, however, make a distinction between the second-rate and the second-hand; and I suggest that it is the failure to make that distinction which has too often misled people into the absurd idea that anything which is not 'new' has to be almost automatically labelled 'cliché'.

'Oh, but we all know what a cliché is!' I hear said. Do we? Below I give a few examples of expressions (and, in a few cases, single words) which might be labelled 'genuine' clichés, all or nearly all of which I have recently heard or found in print. They are, as will be seen, a very mixed bunch indeed.

* *Anchor.* see *Mileage.*
* *Angel*, recording.   An old friend, not often seen out and about these days, though Bernard Levin entertained him in *The Times* of 8 June 1984:

> Would we go back to being young if the recording angel proffered his book and bade us cross out as many years as we pleased?

– which is the sort of question dear old Arthur Benson might have asked himself as he gazed out of his college window in 1905, and got himself lampooned for in the *Cambridge Review*. 'Proffered' and 'bade' are wing-collared words. (Cf. Benson's invariable 'sate' for 'sat'.)

* *Angel*, writes like an.   This has an interesting circular history. Originally used by Garrick of Goldsmith ('Noll . . . wrote like an angel, but talked like poor Poll') in conversation – quite possibly in one of those coffee houses which people used in those days as much as they now use pubs. Having for nearly two centuries been an acceptable literary allusion, with or without the second part of it, and applied to any good writer, it has been hopelessly overworked and has been put out to grass, being heard only in Fleet Street pubs, which are the sort of place it may well have started in, but now with a sense of shame at its banality – a sad end to a grand old cliché. Cannot be used for camp purposes.

Since writing the above I see Philip Purser using the phrase in the *Sunday Telegraph*, which just goes to show how wrong one can be about these things. Look homeward, angel, now . . . Have I not said that it is the context that matters?

* *Attack*, savage.   An automatic doublet, used by journalists and rabblerousers, for any sort of attack, physical or verbal. 'Savage' has now lost most of its force. 'We have witnessed the effect on people of de-industrialisation, privatisation, homelessness and the savage cut-backs in health care.' (Arthur

Scargill, National Union of Mineworkers' President, in *Sunday Times*, 9 September 1984).
* *Awful.* A word used by smart writers to describe someone they know nothing about. Entirely meaningless.

> This bungling management (including, for a time, Jilly Cooper's awful husband Leo) never quite managed to entirely destroy the company...
> – David Cameron in *City Limits*, April 6–12, 1984.

This *may* actually just mean something, but we have to guess. Probably either 'Leo Cooper, whom I have not met' or 'Leo Cooper, who ignored me at a party we were at'. See also *Private Eye, passim*.

Further down the same paragraph, incidentally, we find an example of fashionable periphrasis which has had a good run:

> Then Peter Mayer, he of Penguin, arrived on the scene with chequebook in hand.

This is a perfectly legitimate alternative way of saying 'made an offer', in the ballad-toting tradition, but is hardly ever found in 'good' writing. (See below under *Purse strings*.)
* *Bike*, mind my. One of the catchphrases in Jack Warner's wartime show, 'Garrison Theatre', invariably used by him on entry, and demonstrating our almost universal pleasure in hearing for the hundred and first time what has already delighted us a hundred times before. The show was enjoyed by lowbrows and highbrows alike. Its utter reliability helped people stay sane on the home front in wartime.
* *Bike*, on yer. This was a charming way of inviting a friend to leave the premises, until taken up for political purposes by Norman Tebbitt; it is now very nearly spent.
* *Bottom line.* An Americanism. In Britain, meaning the most

important part of an argument or aspect of a situation, it comes in the nose-picking class.

* *Cake*, let them eat.   Variants of this have kept poor Marie Antoinette turning in her grave (see *Grave*) for many generations, but there is still some mileage (see *Mileage*) to be got out of it. (Mrs Thatcher, of the families of striking miners: 'Let them eat coke.') My class 9.

* *Caring; caring community*.   Still going strong, in the sense that it is much used. But 'caring', in its various connections, has had most of the blood drained out of it, since it has been taken over by the social service departments of local government offices, and used to describe their function, in a neutral way, so that it is nearer, say, the colourless word 'medicine' than the more emotive 'healing'. Attempts to restore its emotive content risk scorn, as happened to the wretched Church leader called to give evidence in the Palumbo inquiry (see page 39), who declared that the plan to provide a dusty square for pedestrians and loafers outside Mr Palumbo's proposed skyscraper 'had much to say about caring'. What the Reverend meant was that the square would be a jolly good public amenity, but he was so moithered by the new language in which the Church now finds itself compelled to spread the Gospel, that he felt he had to use it, and so made a fool of himself.

* *Cart before the horse, the*.   You would think this was dead, having all the marks of an IC, but Partridge dates it from the sixteenth century, and adds: 'Not, I think, a cliché before C. 18.' What makes him think it began to be a cliché in that particular century I have no idea; probably he merely found more instances of it then. Today, one imagines its use to be confined to the sages of the taproom, but not so. I recently came across a good instance from an exemplary writer:

> 'I have a foreign policy, therefore I am' is cart before horse.
> (Colin Welch, *Spectator*, 28 July 1984)

The fact is that it has really become so idiomatic that no one jibs at it. (Another horsy metaphor, by the way.) Also the writer gave it a little fillip by shortening it in a mannered, seventeenth-century way (compare Milton's 'New presbyter is but old priest writ large'). And perhaps he had a pun somewhere inside his head which got out when he wasn't looking. (Cart, Descartes, geddit?) Anyway, there's life in the old nag yet.

* *Cement-mixer.* 'So-and-so talks like a cement-mixer.' Coined by my friend Peter Wilby, far and away the wittiest man in the Gray's Inn Road, about a certain apparatchick of the National Union of Students, who in view of the aptness of the description should in charity remain nameless. I was so pleased with this *mot* and have repeated it so often that it is in sad danger of becoming an instant cliché.

* *Concern*, overwhelming. 'Of overwhelming concern to the entire trade union and Labour movement' (*Guardian* leader, 2 August 1984.) A tired doublet; illustrates the principle that the strongest words lose strength the quickest. By an apparent paradox, great concern has more force than overwhelming concern.

* *Crack of doom.* Partridge said this phrase from *Macbeth* became a cliché in about 1920. How he dated it, I don't know. Anyway, it appeared in the *Daily Express* on 1 August 1984, over the byline of that paper's political correspondent, Peter Hitchens, who was writing about a proposal to put limits on the length of backbenchers' speeches. Mr Kinnock's speeches, said Mr Hitchens, 'stretch out to the crack of doom'. In the same piece we have '100 novice MPs straining in the slips' and 'marathon men like Labour's John Golding'. The *Express* retained, even after it reached its degenerate days, an elegant command of cliché, Mr Hitchens, in particular, handling the stock with great assurance. The *Express* likes punning clichés, too. But the real masters of the punning cliché are those who write the captions for the topless dolly-birds in the *Sun*, *Daily Star* and elsewhere. A venerable art form.

* *Disaster*, road to.   'Slowly but always inevitably, Mr Booth takes his character down the dark road to disaster and oblivion.' (Eric Redfern, drama critic, *Eastbourne Gazette*, 25 July 1984). Pure, straight automatic writing with no frills. When the writer sleeps, the reader snoozeth also . . .

In the same column Mr Redfern offers us 'with a vengeance' and 'the doubting Thomas brigade'. Eric Partridge, who disliked the use of 'Holy Matrimony' outside church, would not approve of Doubting Thomas in this context. However, I suppose that soon enough Doubting Thomas, like Peeping Tom, will become detached from his origins, both St John's Gospel and Lady Godiva being generally forgotten, except by churchgoers and the inhabitants of Coventry, though they will continue to live in print. I wonder, even now, how many of Mr Redfern's readers knew who St Thomas was. But perhaps I do them an injustice.

* *Dusky hues*.   Facetious circumlocution which some people would want to put in my class 4 (lapse of taste), but can be made to work well if properly handled, as here by a *Daily Star* journalist discussing the suggestion that there had never been a Black Olympic swimmer winner:

> Is it true, as the sage of the saloon bar claims, that white people naturally float, while those of duskier hues naturally sink? If so, why so? We do not know. And we hope we will be told.

That is nicely done, I would say.

* *End of the day*, at the.   Political cliché popularised by Harold Wilson; worn out in Westminster, but still heard on trains.

* *Environment*.   A vicious word, class 1. 'The area round Ham Lane was being environmentally improved' (*Sunday Express*, 17 August 1984). One trembles for Ham Lane. Developers and even local planning authorities who use the word fool either themselves or others with the idea that if something is environ-

mental it must be good, whereas its proper use is quite neutral. The Department of the Environment now qualifies as an Orwellian concept, though not intended as such. The *Sunday Express* journalist quoted above seems to have taken the word seriously, a dismal thought. See Peter Simple, *passim*.
* *Fresh air*, a breath of.   Very stale. 'In Britain we take freedom for granted. But people behind the Iron Curtain discover that life over here is like a breath of fresh air' (*Sun*, 11 July 1984.)
* *Friendship*, altar of.   'Pouring a libation at the altar of friendship', a rich, rich example of pub circumlocutionary, is recorded by cliché-connoisseur S. J. Perelman. Or rather, of what the boozy salesman says to the wife when he gets home. (In the office, it's 'having a snifter with the boys'.)
* *Grave*, turning in his/her.   Survives through its variations, but only just. 'If Beethoven were alive today he would be turning in his grave', etc.
* *Great and good.*   'A "titular degree" – the sort patronisingly dished out to the great and good who have never usually seen the inside of a Cambridge canteen.' (*The Times* Diary, 8 July 1984.)

'A BBC handout for a new pop programme pledges that "each week, a Radio One DJ will attempt a daring and difficult challenge." Like trying to utter a complete and coherent sentence, for example, with at least one word of more than one syllable? (NB: The great and good Simon Bates, of course, must be exempted from these strictures ...)' – *Daily Star* leader column, 30 July 1984.

Always ironic, I thought, until I read the *Daily Star* leader, where I am almost certain it is 'straight'. Context, once again, is all.
* *Hell*.   In popular newspaper diction this is an adjective. 'The misery of living in a London hell hostel could soon be over for hundreds of families' (*Daily Star*, 3 May 1984). 'Hell Voyage of Snubbed Boat People' (*Daily Express*, 30 July 1984).

* *Insight*, fascinating.   The least fascinating insights are those which are described as such. An obvious class 3 cliché.

> He gives an authoritative and fascinating insight into the debate on the role of the police and describes the conflicts and changes which have fuelled the controversy over the past 25 years ... John Alderson looks at the problems of policing not just from the point of view of criminal justice, but also within the wider context of social order in Britain today.
> (Dust-jacket blurb for John Alderson's *Law and Disorder*, Hamish Hamilton, 1984)

One can almost hear the blurb-writer saying to himself or herself: 'What on earth can I say about this book?' In the end he/she solves the problem by saying nothing. Note also 'fuelled', a hateful word, and 'wider context', another class 3 cliché. The wretched author deserved better than this. (Don't tell me he wrote it himself.)

* *Irony*, gentle.   Used by writers in a hurry, for whom there are only two kinds of irony: one makes you laugh, the other cry. If you laugh it's gentle, if you cry it's bitter. Meanwhile, the reader neither laughs nor cries, but begins to doze.

> The whole façade has a gallant, festive appearance, not without a tinge of gentle irony.
> (Roger Scruton, *The Times*, August 1984)

* *Life*, changing scenes of.   The longest circumlocutionary phrase known to me was perpetrated by the hymn-writers Tate and Brady, who at the beginning of the eighteenth century translated the Greek word *aei* (always) as

> Through all the changing scenes of life
> In trouble and in joy.

* *Local difficulty*, a little.   First made popular by Harold Macmillan. Still acceptable, as camp cliché, and still to be found in political leaders, etc. Already a camp expression, come to think of it, when Macmillan used it.
* *Log*, falling off a.   I had thought never to have seen this IC in print again – hardly anyone would think of using it even in speech – till I came across this sentence in *City Limits* for April 6–12, 1984:

> Now, of all the people you might expect should be able to wangle their way into the hallowed columns of *The Times* as easy as falling off a log it ought to be Messrs Berlin, Moore, Gowing etc.

This is an example of the pop-cynical, or 'wise-guy' style. Note 'hallowed columns'; earlier in the paragraph we have 'missive' for letter. It's really in a sub-division of the nosepicking class. But the 'log' simile surprised me.
* *Love message*, sizzling.   Another automatic doublet. 'A sizzling love message from Koo Stark to Prince Andrew is on the soundtrack of a controversial new record' (*Sun*, 11 July 1984). This word gets cooler and cooler. Compare 'stunning' and 'staggering'. The latter just means 'big'. 'Doc Martens made a staggering 80,000 boots a week' (*Sun*, same issue).
* *Love tangles*.   'A baby born to a stand-in mother was yesterday at the heart of legal and love tangles' (*Daily Express*, 2 August 1984). Unusual to have the two sorts of tangle in one sentence. Pretty perfunctory really. If this minstrel came to my hall, I'd send him to the kitchen quarters and tell him not to come back.
* *Male embraces the female*, the.   A bit of a nose-picker, this. So coy a witticism could hardly survive long. In a career of listening to chairmen's speeches, I cannot remember having heard it for years. The phrase applies throughout this book, incidentally.

* *Mileage.* No mileage to be got out of this one any more. Conversely, as it were, a large body of circumlocutions flourish in the motor sporting magazines. 'He threw out an anchor' for 'applied his brakes'. 'I ran out of road', etc. A rich seam here.

* *Massive.* A heroic word for big: cf. *giant*, which is used for concrete things like factories ('Last night the giant Ravenscraig steel works was set to become the new flashpoint' – *Daily Star*, 3 May 1984), whereas *massive* is generally applied to abstract things. A favourite word among radical intellectuals, whose struggles on behalf of working-class solidarity are, hopefully, massive. If, however, it is handled properly it can still be effective. 'Her massively authoritative reviews' – Bernard Levin, at memorial service for Rebecca West, 21 April 1983. Levin's oration on that occasion, incidentally, shows that the art of encomium, which I discussed in Chapter Three, need not be regarded as dead, so long as the encomiast is not afraid to make use of the tradition. 'Her mortal body', Levin's address ended, 'is committed to the earth of the English countryside; her living memory to the safe keeping of those who knew and loved her; and her enduring repute into the hands of the countless generations who will read her, and admire her, hereafter.' The trouble is that most of us *are* afraid of the tradition. Levin's lapidary prose was right for the time and place: that sentence might not unfittingly have been written when St-Martin-in-the-Fields, where the service was held, was being built.

Meanwhile Bernard Levin knows as well as anyone how narrow is the divide between the lapidary phrase that works, and the one that sounds merely pretentious, and how easy it is to end up on the wrong side of it. (See *Angel*; and Levin's work, *passim*.)

* *Material.* Formerly purely an academic cliché: 'Is he scholarship material?' Now on general release. 'Lewes people are not Carnival material' (*Sussex Express*, 17 August 1984).

* *Meaningful.* Meaningless word. Has been mocked so much that it is now very seldom heard, and it is a long time since I have spotted one. Peter Simple of the *Daily Telegraph* did much to hasten its departure with the reported statements of trendy Church leaders who were fond of saying that something or other was relevant to the age we live in, in a very real and meaningful sense. Now respectable only among philosophers, for whom it does have a precise function. Long before they got hold of it, however, it was surely used by novelists in a different sense: a 'meaningful glance' was a glance which, though unaccompanied by words, had much to say, whether affectionate, conspiratorial or angry. Were not people often throwing each other such glances?

* *No way.* 'There is no way we can accept the management's offer.' The phrase is most often heard in trade union circles now, but I have heard it used by what appeared to be middle-class commuters. They may have been trade union officials, but I don't think so.

* *One thing is certain.* Leader-writer's standby, very popular at one time. All leader-writers have the same task: to explain, however briefly, what it's about, and to tell the reader what the paper thinks about it. 'One thing is certain' bridges the gap between the two nicely, especially in heavy leaders where there is a great deal of explaining to do and the leader-writer has got bogged down. They have been pretty well laughed out of it by now, but it can still be found elsewhere:

> One thing is certain: by the time England join the fight for the real Ashes in Australia in the winter, they will be battle hardened.
>
> (*Daily Express*, 1 August 1984)

'Battle hardened', incidentally, has an echo in advertising copy: compare 'heat toughened', 'wax protected', etc.

* *Pint-sized.* Literary circumlocution in the classic tradition

(white-armed, fair-girdled, many-wiled, etc.), but only in popular journalism. 'The pint-sized superstar' – Olga Maitland, in *Sunday Express*, 13 May 1984, of Dudley Moore, a small actor.

* *Pit*, bottomless.   'The unforeseen developments in medical technology meant that a bottomless pit of demand was opened up.' (*Guardian* leader, 13 August 1984.) Clumsy use of an old-timer.

* *Privacy*, invasion of.   Sunbathing housewife, peeped at by helicopter pilots: 'The people aboard were having a good ogle. It was a blatant invasion of privacy.' I now forget where I spotted this latter-day Susanna. Invasions of privacy are, of course, like lies; they are always blatant. If Susanna didn't actually use the word, this was only an oversight on her part, and it was natural that the reporter should supply it.

* *Purse strings*, etc.   'Prices which do not send the purse strings into shock' (Georgina Daly's Restaurant Guide, *Eastbourne Gazette*, 25 July 1984). The pathetic fallacy: a time-honoured device. Nothing wrong with it.

> Come away, come away, Death
> And in sad cypress let me be laid.
> – *Twelfth Night*

The sadness is transferred from the person feeling it to the cypress-wood coffin. Right for Shakespeare, wrong for Daly. Why? Because this sort of writing is out of fashion among good authors, and has fallen into the hands of the smart-alecs and the inadequates. See entries under *Awful* and *Log*, above, for 'wise-guy' writing. Once again, it's all a matter of taste. Another example of 'smartness': 'My lightning schoolboy French gave me an instantaneous translation readout' – this from *Cars and Car Conversions*, February, 1983. In the same article, friends' recommendations to a certain doctor (or 'quack') become 'rave reviews', and when he meets the doctor's attractive assistant he feels 'about as cool and self-confident as an acned 13-year-old with halitosis trying to make it with Joan Collins'. The model, it is almost needless to say, is P. G. Wodehouse, whose stories are full of such tricks. Right for P.G., wrong for the editor of *Cars and Car Conversions?* It seems unfair. Why does David Cameron in *City Limits* make the reader (or this one at any rate) fidget with distaste in a way that the editor of *Cars* does not, and why do we call the said editor an inadequate writer, yet hail Wodehouse as a genius?

The stock answer to such puzzles is that the Wodehouse style is 'played out'. This does not mean that it is no longer to be found: it flourishes in all sorts of places unknown in Wodehouse's day, just as the style of the seventeenth- and eighteenth-century buildings of Greenwich Palace was still being used for city halls, banks and insurance offices in the early twentieth century, the copies vastly outnumbering the originals. (And the copies weren't so good.)

Wodehouse himself could strike an uncertain note at times: I seem to detect a couple too many contrivances of the my-head-hit-the-ceiling sort in his later work, but perhaps I am wrong.

* *Response*, positive. Trade union spokesmen interviewed on television often hope for a positive response from the membership. Comes into either Class 2 (euphemistic) or 3 (self-deluding). Means they'll vote yes.

* *Question-marks.* These invariably hang over people or institutions whose future is in doubt, and are part of the special language of popular newspaper reports. (See Chapter Six.) 'As the multi-millionaire Marquis of Bute buried his 27-year-old daughter Lady Eileen Crichton Stuart yesterday ... a question-mark hung over the future of his son and heir, the Earl of Dumfries.' (*Daily Express*, 16 August 1984.) More often found in provincial newspapers, about an ailing local enterprise.

* *Road*, end of the.   Still much in use in office pubs, facetiously, either about ageing colleagues or by the speaker about himself ('It's the end of the road for me'). Indeed, it is hard to think that it could ever have been used seriously (the speaker expects to be contradicted). But Harry Lauder's song, 'Keep Right on to the End of the Road', used to make audiences cry.

* *Russian roulette*.   Low-grade, semi-instant cliché-metaphor, but still hard at work doing its humble duty by the gutter Press. 'In Britain today it is the trigger-happy union bosses who happily play Russian roulette with working people's livelihoods' (John Vincent in the *Sun*, 11 July 1984).

* *Silence*, deathly.   'The TUC has kept a deathly silence these past 20 weeks' (*Guardian* leader, 2 August 1984). 'The silence has been deafening' – same leader, next sentence. The first variant is a more or less meaningless doublet, with no harm in it. The second is an IC, and merits some groans.

* *Situations*.   'Situation' clichés have attracted so much scorn (particularly in *Private Eye*, which ran a regular column of examples called 'Ongoing Situations') that only the most insensitive speaker or writer would now dare to use them. But I did hear a lovely usage a few years back, which I still treasure. 'We are', said a publisher, 'in a cleft stick situation', thus producing two clichés in the space of five words, an admirable achievement.

* *Streets ahead*.   Very low-grade indeed. Inappropriate for the printed word, to be avoided in letters and conversations. What has doomed it is the heavy emphasis which always has to be put on the word 'streets': *streets* ahead. No metaphor can long bear such a battering. If the emphasis is removed, it becomes far more acceptable: 'When it comes to autobiography, Quennell is a street or two ahead of Lees-Milne.'

* *Time-bomb*.   Much loved by American political cartoonists. Round and black, and suitably inscribed 'Iran' or 'Salvador' or whatever, it is sat on by Presidents and Secretaries of State. I came across a written one not long ago:

> As we have seen from the escalating violence this week, the coal strike is an enormous time bomb ticking away under the feet of the Government and the nation.
> – Paul Johnson, *Daily Mail*, 18 August 1984

(The cartoonists' time bombs, incidentally, never tick. They have sparkling fuses.) Paul Johnson writes with such conviction that he gets away with this ancient machinery, which, again, seems somehow unfair to others who try the same thing and produce only squibs.

* *Tract for the times.* 'His Penguin book *Education for Tomorrow* was ... very much a tract for the times' (*Daily Telegraph*, obituary of John Vaizey, 20 July 1984). 'Tract for the times' here becomes an adjectival phrase, meaning 'timely and influential'. The 'very much' is rather clumsy, I suggest. But the phrase is inappropriate anyway, since there are plenty of people who know that it was the title of a series of High Church pamphlets launched by Newman in the 1830s. So it's really a rotten way of saying that something is of topical interest, which is about all the obituarist meant.

* *Ugandan discussions.* Self-generating cliché, the generator in this case being *Private Eye*, which coined it to describe a sexual liaison. My class 2.

* *Utterly reliable.* A harmless doublet. 'Utterly' is here simply a variant of 'totally', but more idiomatic.

* *Violence.* A Humpty-Dumpty word. 'The violence of poverty' – Arthur Scargill, president of the National Union of Mineworkers, in an answer to charges that he was condoning violent picketing during the 1984 miners' strike. In this sense violence is something – anything – which outrages whoever is using the word, and need not be physical. I had imagined it must be an ignorant mistake for 'violation' – i.e., that it was thought of as having both concrete and abstract meanings, but I don't think so. Militant student leaders at the London School of Economics, who had torn down some internal gates at the School in 1969, excused themselves on the ground that 'putting up the gates in the first place was itself an *act* of violence'. This is less a cliché than an item of political jargon.

* *Wafer thin.* Automatic doublet given new life in felicitous *Daily Mail* headline, 31 August 1984: '... in Forsyth's ice cream saga laughs are wafer thin'. My class 9.

* *Wax philosophical.* This is just about the only thing people do wax these days. An idiom with ironic undertones, though I am not sure that the author of this example meant to be ironic:

> Meanwhile, the colliers sometimes wax philosophical about their fate.
> – Paul Routledge, *The Times*, 8 August 1984

* *Woefully inadequate.* 'Woefully' is called an 'intensifier' by grammarians, lexicographers and suchlike. Here it is a lazy word, doing practically no work at all:

> The Daily Telegraph has a good crossword and excellent foreign news coverage but is woefully inadequate in reporting most aspects of modern society, which it has simply failed to notice. (*Daily Mail*, 18 August 1984, in an editorial puff for the *Daily Mail*. Another example of automatic writing.)

* *Wolf,* cry. Amazingly resilient. Still effective. 'In the face of all this progress, the rail unions' federation is choosing this time to persuade people in this industry to listen to cries of wolf and incitements to suicidal behaviour.' (Railway spokesman, quoted in *The Times*, August, 1984). Has more force than a mere false alarm, which is all it means. But the original young

shepherd cried 'Wolf' once too often, so that people stopped listening. Perhaps the same will happen to this phrase one day.

Notes

Introduction

1 Walter Gropius, *The New Architecture and the Bauhaus* (Faber, 1935) p. 37
2 Myles na gCopaleen, *The Best of Myles* (MacGibbon & Kee, 1968) p. 227

Chapter One

1 Eric Partridge, *A Dictionary of Clichés*, 3rd edn, 1947 (RKP, 1940) p. 2
2 A. L. and I. L. Sells, *Thomas Gray* (Allen & Unwin, 1980)
3 Joseph Spence, *Anecdotes, Observations and Characters of Books and Men* (written mostly between 1728 and 1744

and ed. S. W. Singer, 1820: described by Singer as 'A Lounging Book for an idle hour')
4. In *Lives of the Poets*.
5. Roger Ascham, *The Scholemaster*, 1570. (Ed. Edward Arber, Birmingham, 1870)
6. Richard Mulcaster, *Positions*, 1581. (Ed. R. H. Quick, Longmans, 1888)
7. J. H. Badley, *Memories and Reflections* (Allen & Unwin, 1955) p. 50
8. See W. A. C. Stewart and W. P. McCann, *The Educational Innovators, 1750–1880* (Macmillan, 1967)
9. David Shayer, *The Teaching of English in Schools, 1900–1970* (RKP, 1972)
10. Nicholas Bagnall (ed.), *New Movements in the Study and Teaching of English* (Temple Smith, 1973)
11. Leslie Stratta, John Dixon and Andrew Wilkinson, *Patterns of Language* (Heinemann Educational, 1973) p. 17
12. Harold Rosen with Nancy Martin, 'Writing Prose', in Brian Jackson (ed.), *English versus Examinations* (Chatto, 1965)
13. A. B. Clegg (ed.), *The Excitement of Writing* (Chatto, 1964) p. 5, p. 9
14. Randolph Quirk, *The Use of English*, 2nd edn, 1968 (Longmans, 1962) p. 249

Chapter Two

1. C. B. Cox and A. E. Dyson, *The Black Papers on Education* (Davis-Poynter, 1971) p. 85
2. Edmund Burke, *A Philosophical Inquiry into the Origin of our Ideas of the Sublime and Beautiful*, 1756. (Cassell's edn, with introduction by Henry Morley, p. 17)
3. *Encyclopaedia Britannica*, (Cambridge, 1911) 11th edn, Vol XXVII, p. 829. [My italics.] For a general discussion of

eighteenth-century aesthetics, see Hussey, *The Picturesque* (1927)
4 David Martin (ed.), *Anarchy and Culture* (RKP, 1969) pp. 6 ff.
5 Walter Gropius, *The New Architecture and the Bauhaus*, tr. P. Morton Shand. New edn, 1965 (Faber, 1935) p. 19
6 Nikolaus Pevsner, *An Outline of European Architecture*, 1963 edn (Pelican, 1942) p. 363. For Ruskin, compare John Unrau, *Looking at Architecture with Ruskin* (Thames & Hudson, 1978)
7 Harry Fieldhouse, *Everyman's Good English Guide* (Dent, 1982) p. 110
8 *An Outline of European Architecture* (1942 edn) p. 146
9 Gropius, p. 38
10 Pevsner, *Pioneers of Modern Design* (Faber, 1963; Pelican edn, 1975) p. 216
11 For a tirade on this last point, see Tom Wolfe, *From Bauhaus to Our House* (Cape, 1982)

Chapter Three

1 *A Language for Life*, Report of A Committee of Inquiry under Lord Bullock (HMSO, 1975)
2 *The Alternative Service Book* (Hodder, 1980)
3 Lisle March-Phillipps and Bertram Christian (eds.), *Some Hawarden Letters 1878–1913* (Nisbet & Co, 1917) pp. 185–6
4 Unpublished. I am grateful to Mr William Haly for permission to quote from these papers.
5 R. Brimley Johnson (ed.), *The Letters of Hannah More* (Bodley Head, 1925) p. 76
6 At Eardisley, Herefordshire.
7 George Somes Layard (ed.), *Sir Thomas Lawrence's Letter-Bag* (George Allen, 1905) p. 214

8 John Brown and D. W. Forrest (eds.), *Letters of Dr John Brown* (A. & C. Black, 1909) p. 296
9 Lady Strachey (ed.), *Letters of Edward Lear* (T. Fisher Unwin, 1907) p. 183
10 Strachey, p. 215
11 Brown, p. 191
12 Brown, p. 184. 'To my patron and wife – to thee, my Catherine! Beautiful, pious, always most dear, as fleeting as the breath of day, the fugitive shadows.'

Chapter Four

1 Keith Waterhouse, *Office Life* (Michael Joseph, 1978)
2 *The Times*, 24 March 1984
3 W. S. Bristow, *Spiders* (King Penguin, 1947) pp. 26–7
4 S. J. Perelman, *The Ill-Tempered Clavichord* (Max Reinhardt, 1953)
5 In *The Ill-Tempered Clavichord*.
6 Perelman, *Westward Ha! or Around the World in Eighty Clichés* (Simon & Schuster, 1948) p. 9
7 *Westward Ha!*, p. 29
8 Jerome K. Jerome, *The Idle Thoughts of an Idle Fellow* (Leadenhall Press, 1886) pp. 102–3
9 Jerome, p. 87
10 Jerome, p. 67
11 Jerome, p. 76
12 See Frances Donaldson, *P. G. Wodehouse: A Biography* (Weidenfeld, 1982)
13 P. G. Wodehouse, *Mr Mulliner Speaking* (Herbert Jenkins, 1929) p. 13
14 *Mr Mulliner Speaking*, p. 34
15 P. G. Wodehouse, 'Sticky Wicket at Blandings', in *Plum Pie* (Herbert Jenkins, 1966) Coronet edn, 1978, p. 50
16 The same, p. 53

17 In *Nothing Serious* (1950). Reprinted in *Plum Pie* (Coronet edn) p. 162
18 *Mr Mulliner Speaking*, p. 151
19 P. G. Wodehouse, *Much Obliged, Jeeves* (Barrie & Jenkins, 1971) p. 32
20 P. G. Wodehouse, 'Jeeves and the Unbidden Guest', in *Carry On, Jeeves* (Herbert Jenkins, n.d.) pp. 75–6

Chapter Five

1 Randolph Quirk, *The Use of English* (1962 edn) pp. 220–1
2 A. C. Benson, *From a College Window* (Smith Elder, 1906) p. 38
3 David Newsome, *From the Edge of Paradise* (Murray, 1980) p. 171
4 In *Howard's End.*
5 *From a College Window*, p. 94
6 Hugh Walpole, *The Inquisitor* (Macmillan, 1935) p. 410
7 Thomas Hardy, *The Mayor of Casterbridge*, 1895 (Macmillan's Pocket edn, 1906) p. 31
8 To divide all modern fiction into 'mainstream' and 'other' is, of course, much too simple.

Chapter Six

1 Myles na gCopaleen, *The Best of Myles* (MacGibbon & Kee, 1968) pp. 201 ff.
2 II Peter, i. 19
3 Butcher and Lang's translation, more or less.
4 Christopher Walker in *The Times*, May 24, 1984.
5 *Ars Poetica*, tr. H. Rushton Fairclough (Heinemann, 1926)
6 In *The Old Familiar Faces*.

7 B. F. Cook, *Greek and Roman Art in the British Museum* (BM Publications, 1976) p. 59
8 Pope's translation of Homer is the most inaccurate, but still the best.
9 Leslie Stephen, *Alexander Pope* (Macmillan, 1880) Library edn, 1911, p. 65
10 In *The Traveller*, 1764.
11 *The Art of Preserving Health*, 1744. Not, of course, poetry, but prose (very prosaic, too) with poetic devices stuck on.
12 Herbert Lindenberger, *On Wordsworth's Prelude* (Princeton U. P., New Jersey, 1963) p. 297. I am not concerned here with which is the better version of *The Prelude*. No one today would vote for the 1850 re-write.
13 J. W. Hales and F. J. Furnivall (eds.), *Bishop Percy's Folio Manuscript* (3 vols, 1867-8), Vol I, p. xx. It is only fair to add that many (most?) modern poets would agree with Furnivall; they would reject the idea that poetry has a special language. Thus Robert Graves wrote in 1969 of 'the other side of the great 1911 watershed, when poets were still bound to a liturgical diction and vocabulary which now reads phoney and hypocritical, however honest the material'. (*Between Moon and Sun: Selected Letters 1946-72*, ed. Paul O'Prey, Hutchinson, 1984.) The ballad form was taken up again (though in conditions very different from those in which it was first used) because it was regarded as 'pure' poetry: compare some Post-Impressionists' obsession with primitive art, for similar reasons. But each poet has his or her own special *voice*, the reverse of a shared tradition.

Meanwhile, by an apparent paradox, when poetry was public property, and popular, as it was in ancient Greece, it had a special vocabulary and diction of its own – whereas many 'modern' poets, who shrink from poetic diction of any sort and believe in using common speech, still produce verse which is both private and unpopular.

14 Pamphlet on the Ballad Society, bound in with Bishop Percy.
15 Pope in *The Rape of the Lock* satirised the whole machinery when he personified Coffee.
16 Compare *Iliad*, ix. 2:
   > While Fear, pale comrade of inglorious flight,
   > And heaven-bred horror, on the Grecian part,
   > Sat on each face, and saddened every heart.
   >   (Pope's translation)
17 Pope's translation.
18 *The Journal* (Institute of Journalists, December 1939) p.19
19 In the summer of 1984 the south transept of York Minster was struck and its roof burned out. A surprisingly large number of people attributed this misfortune to God's wrath against the newly-consecrated Bishop of Durham, whom they regarded as a heretic.
20 Bishop Percy, Vol I, p. 299
21 By 1984 the *Daily Star* had evidently found the strain of finding 'facts' to fit the stories a bit too much for it. It was reserving its four centre pages for a Mills & Boon romance. For more about the gutter Press, see Henry Porter, *Lies, Damned Lies and Some Exclusives* (Chatto, 1984)

Chapter Seven

1 Jacques Barzun (tr.), *Flaubert's Dictionary of Accepted Ideas* (Max Reinhardt, 1954)
2 Gustave Flaubert: letter to Louis Bouilhet, 4 September 1850 (Barzun's translation). Francis Steegmuller has 'conventional morality' for 'sound convention' (French: *la convention générale*).
3 Weidenfeld, 1982
4 Weidenfeld, 1980

5 Barzun, pp. 6–7
6 Barzun, p. 9
7 See *Iliad*, i. 599: 'And unquenchable laughter (*asbestos gelōs*) stirred the blessed gods.' Flaubert's diners would have known this line of Homer's, or pretended to.
8 Which was pretty blasphemous, as it was most notably applied to Jesus.
9 For more of this, if you can take it, see Nigel Rees, *The Joy of Clichés: a Complete User's Guide* (Macdonald, 1984), particularly pp. 22 ff. Most of Mr Rees's clichés are spoken. But he also has a nice collection of authors' acknowledgements in the fronts of books, publishers' blurbs, letters to newspapers, etc. See also another, rather more indiscriminate cliché-gatherer, Keith Miles, *The Finest Swordsman in All France* (Sphere, 1984). The real wizard of the spoken cliché, as well as of professional jargonspeak, is the incomparable Posy Simmonds of the *Guardian*.
10 *Report of the Director General*, 1961 (Unesco, Paris), p.161
11 Richard Hoggart, *Only Connect*, 1971 Reith Lectures (Chatto, 1972) pp. 84–5
12 Including: *Implementation of research; developmental goals; innovative patterns*, and, of course, *the human factor*.
13 Both quotations are from actual letters.
14 From Beverley Raphael, *The Anatomy of Bereavement* (Hutchinson, 1984)
15 *Royal Commission on Local Government in England, 1966–1969* (HMSO, 1969) Vol III, p. 178
16 G. P. Meredith, 'Communication and Education', in George Z. F. Bereday and Joseph A. Lauwerys (eds.), *The Year Book of Education, 1960* (Evans Bros, 1960) p. 55
17 John Hambley, 'Diversity: a Developmental Perspective', in Ken Richardson and David Spears (eds.), *Race, Culture and Intelligence* (Penguin, 1972) p. 55
18 Tom Lovett, 'An Experiment in Adult Education in the

EPA', in Eric Midwinter (ed.), *Projections* (Ward Lock Educational, 1972) p. 75
19 In his appendix to *Nineteen Eighty-Four*.
20 Orwell, in *Politics and the English Language* (1946), instances the word *democracy*: 'It is almost universally felt that when we call a country democratic we are praising it: consequently the defenders of every kind of regime claim that it is a democracy . . .'
21 See also Kenneth Hudson, *The Language of Modern Politics* (Macmillan, 1978). On a lighter note, see Jeremy Lawrence, *Mix me a Metaphor* (Gentry Books, 1972)
22 J. A. Douglas, *The Relations of the Anglican Churches with the Eastern Orthodox* (Faith Press, 1921) p. 57

Chapter Eight

1 George Orwell, 'Politics and the English Language', in *Collected Essays* (Secker & Warburg, 1961) p. 351
2 Orwell, p. 350
3 Susan M. Lloyd (ed.), *Roget's Thesaurus of English Words and Phrases* (Longman, 1982) p. xii
4 Orwell, p. 345
5 Much the same point is made by Ernest Gowers, *The Complete Plain Words* (HMSO, 1954, revised 1958) p. 77
6 Philip Howard falls into the same error in a witty chapter on clichés in his *The State of the Language* (Hamish Hamilton, 1984). (He even borrows Partridge's joke about hackneyed phrases which are knock-kneed and spavined, as well as his remark about idioms which have been so indiscriminately used that their points are blunted, but, strangely, forgets to tell us where he got them from.) He does, however, concede that clichés are there to be used when needed.
7 Partridge, p. 4

8 Gowers, *The Complete Plain Words*, p. 57
9 Gowers, p. 106
10 Barbara Jones, *Water-Colour Painting* (A. & C. Black, 1960)
11 Ezra Pound, *How to Read* (1931)
12 T. S. Eliot, *Poetry and Drama*, Theodore Spencer Memorial Lecture (Faber, 1951)
13 Fay Weldon, *Letters to Alice* (Michael Joseph/Rainbird, 1984) p. 12